The CURIOUS CHRISTIAN

HOW DISCOVERING WONDER
ENRICHES EVERY PART OF LIFE

BARNABAS PIPER

B&H
PUBLISHING GROUP
NASHVILLE, TENNESSEE

978-1-4336-9192-8

Published by B&H Publishing Group
Nashville, Tennessee

Dewey Decimal Classification: 155.2
Subject Heading: CHRISTIAN LIFE \ CURIOSITY \
HUMAN BEHAVIOR

1 2 3 4 5 6 7 8 • 21 20 19 18 17

The CURIOUS CHRISTIAN

Dedication

For my mother.

I remember lying on top of the luggage in the back of our Chevy Caprice "Woody" station wagon on the endless drive from Minnesota to Georgia and listening to you read adventure stories loud enough for me to hear all the way in the back and reading so well I forgot how bored I was.

I remember sitting in the kitchen while you made dinner and listening to *Fresh Air* on NPR over the sounds of my growling stomach. I never knew what was happening, but I knew it was important.

I remember the soothing tones of Garrison Keillor's voice and the quirky, dry humor of Lake Wobegon as you listened to the *Prairie Home Companion*.

I remember you helping me with science and history projects and being much more enthralled with the topics (especially history) than I was.

I remember shelf upon shelf of mysteries by Agatha Christie, P. D. James, and others. And what says curiosity like a love of mystery?

I remember you giving me a chance to do the things I loved and invest in my interests even when it meant freezing your toes off at snowy

November football games or weekly trips to the Franklin Library during the summer.

I remember how you read all the plaques at museums and Civil War battle fields. I was so bored. Now I bore my own children.

I remember you making a home for more than thirty years in the same, diverse, sometimes rough, never boring, Phillips Neighborhood of Minneapolis and showing me how to love its numerous people and cultures.

I remember your love of learning and travel and your insatiable desire to understand and discover. You asked so many questions!

I remember you *teaching*—teaching me, teaching my siblings, teaching at church, teaching about God's Word, about history, about literature, about culture.

Now I hope that you can pull this book from your expertly packed carry-on as you sit on a 747 destined for Taiwan, Sweden, New Zealand, or Zambia. I hope you can see how your curiosity, your investment, your example has shaped me and fed these pages. I wrote the words, but so many of the ideas are yours.

Thank you.

Contents

Acknowledgments

I'D LIKE TO THANK everyone who gave me blank stares when I said I was writing a book on curiosity. You were a consistent reminder of exactly why I was writing.

To the many friends who didn't give blank stares but rather asked insightful, pointed, *curious* questions—thank you. You were the crucial balance to the blank stares, my reminder that curious people exist and want to learn and ask and grow.

Though he can't hear me and will never read this, Oscar Peterson deserves thanks for his music. It carried me through the writing of this book while keeping my spirits up.

To the innumerable influences on my own curiosity—the authors, teachers, podcasters, musicians, actors, playwrights, friends, and who-knows-who-else—I do not know how to thank you because your web of influence cannot be untangled. And for that I am grateful. Your complex, varied, and constant influence has helped shape me.

To the team at B&H—this book has been a challenging process in a challenging time of life, and you have never failed to be encouraging and enthusiastic about it. For an author that is fresh air and cool water. Thank you.

Introduction

HOW RANDOM, A BOOK on curiosity. Is "curiosity" even a thing? Can it actually be defined or described? Is it something people can conscientiously do or respond to? It seems like a trait some people—usually children or weird people—have and others don't.

If curiosity is a trait received passively at birth, then what is the point of reading an entire book on something about which you have little control? That's like reading at length about height or hair color. Curiosity just doesn't seem like the kind of idea that's *actionable*, and that's what most people want in a book—something to read that tells them what to do. But curiosity is an actionable concept, and the book you're holding might surprise you with how much practical wisdom is available to curious Christians.

I'm a curious person. As a curious person, the very questions posed above and others like them are why I think a book on curiosity matters! You may not think of yourself as particularly curious, but don't sell yourself short. Do you find yourself asking questions often? That's not a sign of being dumb; it's a sign of being curious. Do you find yourself wondering about seemingly random things as you drive down the road or go for a jog? That's not daydreaming; it's curiosity. Do you see little, quirky, odd things about everyday life that others might miss? That's not odd at all; it's curiosity.

For curious people, what appears to be random catches our attention. What we must explore is whether or not it is really random. Or might there be something more under the surface? In almost every case, what seems random or odd is not really; there's more to the story that just isn't obvious at first glance. It is "randomness" that inspired these pages. Vagueness and intangible ideas captured my mind and moved me to try to order them and give them flesh.

When most people see something that makes little sense to them, instead of engaging it, they cringe, cross the street, and hustle on their way, leaving it for someone else to deal with. They treat ideas or events that "are not really in their wheelhouse" the same way, whether it's art, sports, science, politics, current events, or whatever. Basically, most people avoid most complex ideas and happenings that do not directly relate to their immediate needs or interests. They go about their business living in their narrow view of life.

Going about life in this manner is what I call "uncuriosity," and it has consequences. Severe ones. It dramatically affects how we see the world and all its inhabitants. I unpack these side effects further in chapter 3, but here is a summary.

Side Effects of "Uncuriosity"

Binary Thinking

There are two kinds of people in the world: Those who divide everything into two groups and those who don't. Binary thinking takes the grays of the world and insists they are either black or white. It responds to sensitive and complex situations with either/or thinking and in the end creates far more issues than it resolves.

Missed Connections

Most people in the world are strangers to us. We do not know them and because we do not know them we fear them, for the unknown and the different are scary. Instead of seeing the potential for gaps to be bridged, uncuriosity sees the gaps as protection from the foreign and frightening.

Depleted Friendships

True friendships are among the rarest of commodities. We have buddies and coworkers and neighbors but not so many friends. We lack connection with others because we fear letting them close or digging into their lives. Uncuriosity says such behavior is risky, messy, and terribly uncomfortable. It is much simpler and neater to leave people in the acquaintance zone.

Love Lost

Marriage is powerful and fragile, and it is incredibly difficult too. Marriage takes remarkable effort because love gives in to the inertia of life. It stalls and stales unless we intentionally, passionately, actively fight to keep it going and living and sparking. Only curiosity will do this because it recognizes the unknown depths of the spouse and the relationship and seeks to learn and love it all. Uncuriosity sits idly by and lets the love grow still, cold, and dead.

God Is . . . ?

Some of us know much of God, but how many of us have a vibrant relationship with God? We know the phrase but not the reality. We know of God but we don't know God. In the same way that friendships never start and marriages fade, we fail to draw close or stay close to God. Because we are uncurious—uncurious about the depths of His goodness and the mysteries of His ways. Our uncuriosity settles for flannel graph depictions of God instead of relentlessly and eagerly seeking to know Him.

I Don't Care

The world is so much larger than us. It holds the lives of seven billion unique image bearers of God from tens of thousands of cultures and millions of subcultures. It is beautiful and terrible and majestic and sublime. And none of this matters to the uncurious because all he can think about is what's for lunch or when new episodes of *Daredevil* will be on Netflix for his binge-watching pleasure. Uncuriosity not only doesn't care. It cannot.

Only curiosity will recognize that what appears complex, complicated, or random and disconnected is, in fact, more connected at a deeper level to things that do matter to us than we've ever considered. What if sports actually are relevant, say, to your interest in family life? Or what if politics is somehow connected to your interest in the arts? What if all of life is a web of truth that connects us to other people and to God? What if the experience we cold-shouldered was the connecting point to a group of people who might bring out the best in us and bless us in untold ways? What if that idea we avoided holds a kernel of truth that might grow into a vibrant concept of God that we've never encountered before?

Only curiosity will lead to such a discovery. Curiosity *is* actionable. In fact, it can be a mind-set we have all the time that feeds and drives all our actions. In the chapters that follow, I will do my best to show how curiosity is one of the most significant ways we have to be image bearers of God, how it can deepen and expand our relationships with others, how it can lead us to an entirely more significant impact on society, and how it will lead us deeper into a beautiful relationship with God for all time.

Curiosity leads to discovery of great truth throughout all of life. Without it we tread the same paths to and from work, in and out of relationships, through our churches, across the pages of books and Scripture, all without ever seeing what's really there. We are finite creatures bound by time, space, and mental capacity. But bound or not, we almost never press the limits of those boundaries. Rather we stay safely where we are and miss the wonders God has for us.

My aim is not simply to persuade you to see the value of curiosity. Doing that would be like persuading you to believe the ocean is majestic or a star-filled Northern Minnesota night sky is beautiful. What difference would that make? These things are true whether you recognize them or not. I might be able to succeed, but it would not move you at all. I want to expand your thinking with big ideas, but also leave you with some practical ways to grow in curiosity.

In the end I want you to see that curiosity is more than a mere trait. It is a discipline, a skill, a habit—one that will expand your life in magnificent, if subtle, ways. It isn't a discipline like hygiene or working out that we must do to maintain a decent life. It is so much richer than that! Curiosity is like taking your mind and heart on trips to exotic places to experience things you've never before seen and then returning home to take those you love with you. Curiosity is a lifestyle all its own—a holistic, comprehensive interaction with the world around us and all it holds.

When you finish this book, I want you to have more than *just* a deeper understanding of curiosity. I want you to feel claustrophobic in your current state of life and to see the expanses of truth you could experience instead. And I want you to go about the business of leading a life that is "curiouser and curiouser" all the time, with questions leading to answers, leading to wonder, and even more questions so that the passive, accidental limits you've lived by are entirely rearranged or removed all together.

Part 1

To Be Christian
Is to Be Curious

Chapter 1

Do Grown-Ups Really
Need Curiosity?

"'Curiouser and curiouser!' cried Alice."

"He was a good little monkey and always very curious."

The Curious Case of Benjamin Button

YOU PROBABLY RECOGNIZE AT least one of these lines or stories. And not only do we recognize them, they take us back to a time and place. We can almost hear the voice of our mom, grandpa, or first grade teacher reading to us. We picture where we were sitting as we watched Alice follow the frenetic, worried white rabbit into Wonderland. We hear these words and are transported to childhood.

And that is where curiosity lives for many, in a once-upon-a-time-long-long-ago era. It fits in the time in life when we were turning over stones to look at creepy crawly bugs and exploring every forest like it might be Sherwood resplendent with Robin Hood and Maid Marian.

Curiosity is what filled our imaginations once and got us into a fair bit of trouble too, like that time we picked the lock on our sister's diary, disassembled the toaster, or found the Christmas presents Mom hid at the back of her closet under the old sweaters.

Curiosity is a childish word, but not one that ought to be left in the dusty attic with old teddy bears and G.I. Joes. The thing that made it a part of the best childhood experiences is what makes it so important now, today, as an adult.

Childlike, Not Childish

> The ability to retain a child's view of the world, with at the same time a mature understanding of what it means to retain it, is extremely rare—and a person who has these qualities is likely to be able to contribute something really important to our thinking.[1] —Mortimer J. Adler

Maturity, in the minds of many, means smothering all of childhood with responsibility, ambition, and adulthood. It means being focused, productive, and making a difference in the world. The name Peter Banning won't mean much to most of you until you remember the movie *Hook,* starring the late Robin Williams. Banning, Williams's character, is a hard-driving, successful, fast-talking corporate lawyer who is completely disengaged from his children's lives, especially his son Jack. Since the movie came out twenty-five years ago I feel like I can share the ending without a "spoiler alert" warning. Banning is the adult Peter Pan, and a key element of the story is how he must relearn to have *fun* again. After Captain Hook kidnaps his kids, their lives depend on Peter learning how to be a child again. He must relearn how to be Peter

Pan. His version of maturity, the inability to laugh and joke and play (and food fight and bangarang and crow), could cost him his children.

Banning is the quintessential American adult, overemphasizing the responsibility of adulthood as the essence of maturity. All things silly, light-hearted, and fun are immature. Maturity means big decisions, fiscal management, and a serious outlook on life. While maturity absolutely means being responsible, I beg to differ about whether that is the whole of it. And I have the apostle Paul and Jesus on my side, so I win.

Paul wrote in 1 Corinthians 13:11, "When I was a child, I spoke like a child, I thought like a child, I reasoned like a child. When I became a man, I put aside childish things." It almost reads as if he agrees with that definition of maturity I just gave, but of course we must acknowledge what Jesus had to say too. In Luke 18, Jesus welcomed little children open-armed, even rebuking His disciples who tried to keep them at bay. Jesus said, "Let the little children come to Me. . . . Whoever does not welcome the kingdom of God like a little child will never enter it" (vv. 16–17).

Are these contradictory views of childhood? Not at all. One suffix makes all the difference—"ish." As in child*ish*. Paul wrote about putting away those things that are childish, immature. Childish, in this case, means simplistic, shallow, and generally stupid. We know this because Paul talks about thinking and reasoning and speaking like a child. He is talking about how children process information and are generally incapable of complex thought and timely, wise speech. As the parent of two young children, I can verify that the way children think and speak is far more likely to end up with crayon drawings on the wall, spilled maple syrup, and accusations of being a "poop head" than anything resembling complex problem solving or soul searching.

Jesus, on the other hand, praised that aspect of childlikeness that would humbly, excitedly, wondrously welcome His Kingdom. Think of how children respond to fireworks on the Fourth of July. Their "ooooohs" and "aaaaahs" are the very thing that make explosions in the sky so enjoyable for parents. Think of how excited they get at finding a frog in the creek and the leaping squealing joy when Grandma and Grandpa come to visit. The wonder and merriment and raw enthusiasm kids bring to otherwise mundane experiences reveal the spirit Jesus praises. This is childlikeness, not childishness.

Paul's and Jesus's teachings are two sides of the same coin, two parts of a whole. Maturity means growing out of those aspects of childhood that are selfish, unaware of others and the world, an excuse for sin. It does not mean leaving behind all aspects of childhood; to do so, in fact, arrests the development of our souls. We must hold fast to those aspects to which Jesus alluded.

Curiosity is one of these. Children bubble over with questions. Why is the sky blue? Why does my ice cream cone melt? Why can't I see God? What makes the car go? When's dinner? And all those might be in the space of a single hour of an evening. It's marvelous, if a bit exhausting.

Children's minds never stop working, leaping from thing to thing, endlessly wondering about the world and all that it contains. That isn't childish; it's childlike. And it's something grown-ups have lost along the way.

All that wonder and curiosity we had as children was our very nature. We didn't so much learn it; we just couldn't help it. Somewhere in the midst of aging and "maturing," nurture defeated nature, locked it in the dungeon of history, and left it to die. It started in junior high when we realized being a bright-eyed question asker wasn't cool, continued through high school and college as certain subjects and objective exams were upheld as the righteous standard of learning, and the dungeon door slammed shut when we started our careers and families because responsibility left no room for questions and wonder. We were taught, tacitly and explicitly, that some subjects and hobbies matter while others are childish diversions.

We sought maturity, and curiosity had no place in the version we saw.

Real Maturity

But what if maturity is not, as I mentioned earlier, the smothering of childhood so that we can dutifully (and often morosely) handle the cares of adulthood? What if maturity handles the responsibilities of life with all the care and gravity they deserve but not at the expense of childlikeness?

Healthy maturity is that which knows *when* and *how* to be child-like. A child might interrupt her parents to blurt out a seemingly random question about fruit flies or bodily functions or Barbie dolls or why the iPad won't work because she's too immature to recognize the discourtesy. A mature adult might have the same question but knows when and how to ask it so as not to disrespect or disrupt others.

Children love fairy tales, adventure stories, mystic lands, and heroic characters that launch their imagination and turn a backyard into Middle Earth, a swing set into Hogwarts, a rocking chair into a TIE fighter, and a bunk bed into Captain Hook's ship. Every stick is a wand or weapon and every towel a cape. Children embody their heroes in their play and live out the lives of legends. Mature adults love the same stories, are moved by the same heroes, and lose themselves in the same faraway places but without the towel-capes and slat-board swords. (I'll leave you, dear reader, to interpret what this might mean for Comic-Con and Cosplay fans.) Many of us call these stories "guilty" pleasures. We indulge them privately and feel a bit sheepish about it.

What if they aren't "guilty" but rather just pleasures? What if the places our imaginations take us are actually right where we ought to be, healthy and rich places for our minds and souls?

C. S. Lewis was one of the most brilliant Christian thinkers and writers of the twentieth century. He knew multiple ancient languages, was an expert in classic literature and mythology, and an Oxford professor. He wrote magisterially on the nature of God and the relationship between God and man and was a devastating Christian apologist. His work is just shy of the biblical canon for many believers to this day. In short, C. S. Lewis was a mature adult, intellectually superior to most, and fruitful to the extreme. He is to be emulated and looked up to in many ways. Lewis had this to say regarding maturity and becoming an adult:

> "When I was ten, I read fairy tales in secret and would have been ashamed if I had been found doing so. Now that I am fifty, I read them openly. When I became a man I put away childish things, including the fear of childishness and the desire to be very grown up."[2]

> "The modern view seems to me to involve a false conception of growth. They accuse us of arrested development because we have not lost a taste we had in childhood. But surely arrested development consists not in refusing to lose old things but in failing to add new things? . . . Where I formerly had one pleasure, I now have two."[3]

> "It is usual to speak in a playfully apologetic tone about one's adult enjoyment of what are called 'children's books.' I think the convention a silly one. No book is really worth reading at the age of ten which is not equally (and often far more) worth reading at the age of fifty—except, of course, books of information.

The only imaginative works we ought to grow out of are those which it would have been better not to have read at all."[4]

Well now. That paints things in a different light altogether. One of the greatest, most brilliant, most productive Christians in recent history says that we are to somehow, some way, carry childlikeness into adulthood with us! That, friends, is maturity at its best. Any other form is soulless and dull.

Imagination + Information

> Let our teaching be full of ideas. Hitherto it has been stuffed only with facts.[5] —Anatole France

We draw the line between imagination and information. We grow out of the former to invest in the latter. We decide that the former has value for life while the latter is mere escapism from life. This, Lewis would argue, is where we go wrong. He would say that the collection of information, the pursuit of knowledge, is not enough without the fostering and feeding of imagination as well.

> Logic will get you from A to Z; imagination will get you everywhere.[6] —Albert Einstein

> Without leaps of imagination or dreaming, we lose the excitement of possibilities. Dreaming, after all is a form of planning.[7] —Gloria Steinem

> Reality leaves a lot to the imagination.[8] —John Lennon

Imagination guides and shapes our use of information. If we know all the facts and truths, we are just a static hard drive, a library. Libraries are full of information, stacked high and deep. But what can a library do with all the knowledge it holds? Not a thing. It is a static repository, and that is what we are without imagination. What do we do with information? Where does it apply? How can we do the most good with it? Who knows? The person with imagination, who values the virtues of great heroes and can envision and form a better story, knows. That person is *curious*.

Curiosity and imagination are conjoined twins. With one comes the other. Imagination continually asks "what if," then envisions the possible answers and lets the mind run with possibilities. Curiosity asks just about anything, and *then* explores the answers and presses to figure it out and see what else there is. It pokes and prods. Curiosity gives flesh to imagination. If information is dead on its own, then this is the life force that animates it and moves it to action.

The Spark

Kids need routine, they say. They, being experts, are probably right. Routine reduces anxiety and gives children a sense of security about the shape of life. It offers stability and structure, a well-built life on a firm foundation for little, uncertain minds to learn and grow safely. But children love surprises too. They love the unpredictable and the wild. Adults? Not so much.

Most adults take that routine of childhood and anchor it in a concrete foundation buried deep. We thrive on predictable and we live life as if it all ought to be that way. Isaac Newton declared that every action has an equal and opposite reaction, right? So every action we take should have a clear and foreseeable response. We parent this way. We lead our businesses and churches this way. We relate to our spouses and friends this way. We do *everything* as if it should be predictable. In short, we like to live in a rut of consistency. The same stability that creates an environment for children to grow leads adults to stagnate and deteriorate.

But life isn't predictable, is it? People are crazy. Kids are crazy squared. Nature is nuts. Mix in society, politics, religion, family, and you have a morass of who-knows-what-will-happen-next. How's a mature, levelheaded adult trying to manage life in a reasonable, wise way to survive? *With curiosity.*

Curiosity asks what's next, what now, what if, what about, what's that, who, when, and most especially *why.* It asks and asks and asks in part because it knows a surprise waits and in part because it harkens back to childhood. Children snoop under couch cushions, peek behind dressers, rifle through purses, hide in dark closets, climb trees, poke at ant hills, color on walls, play pranks, and wander off in Target because they just have to know what will happen or what's there. As adults, we see these actions as annoying as often—okay, more often—than we do endearing. But they reveal a spark that every adult needs. Without it, the unpredictability of life will become our enemy and eat us up. With it, we keep growing and developing. Unpredictability becomes opportunity.

> Creativity is just connecting things. When you ask creative people how they did something, they feel a little guilty because they didn't really do it, they just saw something. It seemed obvious to them after a while.[9] —Steve Jobs

The spark of curiosity might light a fuse that launches you into the halls of academia, the pulpit of a church, or an executive boardroom. It's just as likely to propel you into the laundry room, the car-pool lane, or the library. It might take you on a walk in the woods, turn on cartoons, or sit you in front of a pile of Legos. Each one is as valuable as the other and has something unexpected to reveal to you. None is more mature or worthwhile than the others *if* done with that spark of curiosity.

Curiosity seeks the unexpected rather than waiting for it to ambush us. Curiosity produces a proactive life rather than a reactive life. We go on the hunt to discover rather than letting the new and strange come to us, and that is where learning and growth happen. Without curiosity we grow as stale as the open package of saltines at the back of the pantry, and as musty as the forgotten boxes in your grandmother's attic. We become lifeless in our souls and minds and then useless in our life and purpose.

From here I hope to walk in that spirit of discovery, that curiosity, through the following chapters. I want to examine our own lives, our faith and relationship with God. Then we get to explore our connection to other people, both those we love and those we have yet to meet. Beyond that is the frontier of society and culture; what does curiosity have to show us about that? From there we will turn our eyes to the great beyond of eternity in heaven or hell. How might curiosity prepare us for eternity and even affect us in the next life?

If all this sounds a bit wild, like maybe I've overshot just a bit and should have just left curiosity in the care of The Man with the Yellow Hat, I simply implore you to move forward with me. Bit by bit I'll try to peel back the layers of predictable reality to reveal the wonder underneath that God has hidden there. Not all of it, of course, but hopefully enough to hook you. Let the spark of curiosity you once had flare into life again. You never know what wonderful place it might take you.

Chapter 2
Curiosity, Creation, and Culture

We're trying to leverage everything we can to be better at what we do and what God has called us to do.[10] —Andy Stanley

IF YOU'VE BEEN KIND enough to agree that curiosity is a virtue, or at least to explore whether it is—which is in and of itself a form of curiosity, by the way—the natural next question is "where do we start?"

What keeps curiosity from becoming a trivial pursuit, voyeurism, or sinful titillation? Look around you and you'll see plenty of things that seem, well, rather unsavory. On one end of the spectrum the porn industry thrives on people's desire to discover and to explore, a sort of sordid curiosity about sexuality and fantasy. On the seemingly innocent end of the spectrum we can lose ourselves in exploration of hobbies—woodworking, photography, fitness, video games—to the point they become our world and rule every waking thought. Curiosity drives us to these hobbies—all good things—but it is not godly curiosity. The world is full of nastiness and full of people seeking to fill a void in their lives. How does curiosity interact with such things, aspects of a fallen world, without leading to sin itself?

What does curiosity seek? Does it have an objective, an aim?

Yes.

Curiosity seeks truth.

Real, godly truth.

What Is True?

Truth is a difficult thing to define, especially in an era when it's been turned into a choose-your-own-adventure story. Remember those? They were the dumbest things. It's like the writers couldn't decide how to end the story so they just wrote five mediocre endings, one of which was happy and four of which ended after two pages with a gruesome death. Entirely dissatisfying even if you figured how to avoid plunging off a cliff or being eaten by a shark. Fittingly, that's what it's like when we pick our own truth too—a terrible ending.

We don't get to define truth or select it. Instead we must recognize and adhere to it. Truth is what is real, what *is*, but it is more than this—much more. If all we did was look around and determine truth by what we saw, we would end up exactly where we are: in a society where truth shifts, morphs, changes, and loses credibility and value each day. Instead we must recognize that truth expresses reality as it *ought to be*. It is a standard for reality, not just a reflection of what currently exists and happens.

Who determines this standard? Not you or I or scholars or priests or politicians or popes. It emanates from God and is expressed by Him in His word. Or, I should say, His Word. For "the Word was with God, and the Word was God. He was with God in the beginning. . . . The

Word became flesh and took up residence among us. We observed His glory, the glory as the One and Only Son from the Father, full of grace and truth" (John 1:1, 14). For Jesus is the Word of God. He is the "image of the invisible God" (Col. 1:15). Jesus is God's Word incarnate. He is the determiner and the displayer of that which is truly true.

So God the Father sent God the Son, the Word, to live among men as truth embodied. But wait, there's more. (As a rule there's always more when it comes to God. Infinity is like that.) The Son didn't stay on the earth; He ascended to His throne and will return as rightful King. But in the meantime He did something remarkable. He gave us His Spirit, the Holy Spirit, the Spirit of Truth. This Spirit is the revealer of truth, the teacher of truth, and the infuser of truth into untrue hearts.

Yet again, there is more, for God did not send His Spirit with a disembodied message. He gave us His written Word, the Bible. It is these words—this revelation of God's character, creation, plan, and work—that the Spirit makes alive, for the Word is alive.

> For the word of God is living and effective and sharper than any double-edged sword, penetrating as far as the separation of soul and spirit, joints and marrow. It is able to judge the ideas and thoughts of the heart. (Heb. 4:12)

Scripture is not an exhaustive description and explanation of God, for that would be impossible (again, infinity). It does not reveal all of His character or His plans. But it is the essential; Scripture enlivened by the Spirit is precisely what we need to know truth. In it God has revealed precisely what we need to believe, to have faith, to know truth, and to live according to it.

Truth reflects some aspect of God's character and persons—Father, Son, and Holy Spirit, in some way—though no truth in this world can display any of them fully. It displays His plan, work, or creation as He intended it to be and will one day make it again. This is the ultimate real, and while it is a great adventure, we do not choose what it will be. We do not pick the ending or the workings or the plot; the Author does that. Truth is entirely shaped and determined by God. All truth is God's truth and reflects this Trinitarian reality.

Truth in Unexpected Places

> True does not mean factual (though it may be factual); true means accurately reflecting human experience.[11] —Daniel Taylor

Too often we think of "facts" when we hear the word *truth*. We think of verifiable statements. While those are true, they are but a tiny subset of truth. Truth is anything that is from God and reflects God in some way. In this way nature can be true. Art can be true. Craftsmanship can be true. Food can be true. Hard work can be true. Even fiction can be true. Truth can be found at every turn, and in some seemingly unlikely places, even without being a proper fact.

God spoke the world into being. His words, again, bringing life. He voiced an idea and it became a beach, a breaker, a star, and a squirrel. And yet another verbalized thought became a llama, a black lab, and an Aspen tree. He voiced another idea and it became a mountain and a man, and then mankind. God's voice, God's words, created all things.

All of creation resonates with God's voice, sometimes only as echoes faint, distant, and indistinct. It reflects Him in some way, blurry or clear. Nothing exists that was not created by God and sustained by God. Sustained means that every day He keeps it existing. We have a hard time imagining the opposite of this, so we take it for granted. But without God's sustaining power, we would cease to exist. We would not fall down dead. We would not crumble into dust or ashes. We would not melt like wax. We would be erased, all of our matter simply gone. Just as God spoke the world into existence—out of nothing, a total void—with His word, so He keeps it in existence daily with His word. And so the world continues to bear God's mark and echo His divine voice.

And this is not just for the big things, like humans and mountains and oceans. God is echoed in rhythms of music, meter of poems, strokes of brush, taps of a hammer, numbers on a pivot table, laughs with a friend, fantastical fiction, icicles, acorns, sweet tea, oak trees, walleye, alloy metals, espresso, and cirrus clouds. All creation speaks truth about God.

Created Uniquely

The resonance of God's voice in all creation is part of what is called common grace,[12] that kindness of God to reveal significant aspects of Himself and His goodness to all people, whether or not they profess faith in Him. Matthew 5:45 exemplifies this when it says, "For He causes His sun to rise on the evil and the good, and sends rain on the righteous and the unrighteous." Romans 1:20 adds some clarity: "For His invisible attributes, that is, His eternal power and divine nature, have been clearly seen since the creation of the world, being understood through what He has made." Common grace doesn't save, but it does summon. It doesn't declare or explain the saving work of Jesus, but it draws people closer to the Creator, or at least the notion of a Creator. It tugs at people's hearts and minds and makes them wonder, and through wonder comes discovery.

Joe Rigney, in his excellent book *The Things of Earth*, describes creation as communication from God. "Creation is a message, an invitation to be drawn into the divine life, the ecstatic vibrance of the Father, Son and the Holy Spirit."[13] But it is a veiled invitation, one that requires interpretation and a guide. A loon's call and rushing waterfall stir hearts, but to what? For people to enter into that "ecstatic vibrance," something more must be at play. All creation is not equal. All truths are not equally clear and understandable. Common grace, natural revelation, stirs hearts but stops there.

God must have intended something more for some part of His creation. If He truly meant to reveal truth, if He wanted His creative word to be effective, then He must have done something clearer, created something more.

> So God created man in His own image;
> He created him in the image of God;
> He created them male and female. (Gen. 1:27)

Indeed, there it is, at the end of the Bible's creation account. No matter what you believe about the order or time frame of creation, no matter how old you think the earth is or how man evolved or didn't, you must recognize this: God made mankind in His image. He didn't do this for the seas or skies or beast or fowl or flora or fauna. Only people.

What does it mean to be created in God's image? The implications are plentiful, but I will point out two. First, we are unique. God did not make anything else in His image. The angels are not even made in God's image. Hebrews 2:7 explains that man is "lower than the angels," but that angels were not charged with ruling over creation. Only mankind was created to inherit the earth. Christ did not come as an angel or spiritual being. He came as a man, fully human, and we are heirs with Christ unlike any other created species or being. We are mammalian, but not animals. We are biologically similar to apes but not essentially similar. We are created to *do* and to *speak* God's revelation, not just echo it. We *are* the images of God to all the world and to each other.

Joe Rigney does a superb job of expressing the second implication: "Being made in God's image is a vocation, something that we are called by God to do and to be."[14] A vocation, a calling, a work we are to dedicate our lives to. That means it is on purpose and with a purpose, not just a state of being. Our vocation will not be done by accident or with passivity any more than your to-do list at work will complete itself while you take a nap or your infant will feed himself while you watch TV. We must reflect God intentionally, each day.

Creating and Culture

One of the most profound ways humans live our vocation of reflecting God is through creating. Unlike any other beast of the field or bird of the air, people can *make*. We cannot create ex nihilo like God (thus the fact that we are reflecting or echoing), but we can take all that God has created and transform it into useful and beautiful things.

Somewhere along the line someone combined pigmented plants into paint and began to make images on cave walls. Over time people noticed that some wall-decorators made buffalos and warriors that looked more lifelike and vibrant, so they took on the job of painting stories and likenesses. Now the *Mona Lisa* hangs on the wall of the Louvre and my kids splatter pre-packaged watercolor paints all over our table.

> Curiosity about life in all of its aspects, I think, is still the secret of great creative people.[15] —Leo Burnett

One day, thousands of years ago, a woman worked at grinding some grain or skinning a rabbit to cook for dinner, and as she worked she hummed. What did she hum? Just some notes that came to mind subconsciously. No, that one sounded wrong, kind of ugly. Yes, there it is, the right note, the beautiful one. And a song was composed and dissonance was discovered. And now Nashville exists with a musician or five playing in every restaurant and honky-tonks and music labels are scattered across the city.

A man once heaved his pick into the hard, dry earth again and again under the burning sun. How would he till enough soil and transport enough water to his little garden patch for his crops to grow and feed his family? He thought about a nearby stream and wondered, *Yes . . . I could dig a trench from there to this little patch.* The ground would be softened and the seeds watered so they could grow. And now as we drive across Indiana, Iowa, or Kansas, we see combines the size of small houses harvesting crops irrigated by the acre with miles of pipes. Enough to feed millions of people.

Once doctors bled patients. They put leeches on them to suck out the poison. They sprinkled them with the blood of animals to ward off the evil. They used rusty implements with unwashed hands to do surgery while patients bit rags or sticks until they passed out from the pain to keep from grinding their teeth or chomping their tongues. A forty-five-year-old was a village elder, and a seventy-year-old was mystically or magically old. But this week I took my daughter to a sparkling clean pediatrician's office replete with fish tank in the waiting room and *Sponge Bob Square Pants* on TV. After thirty minutes, a throat swab, and signature, we were on our way to the pharmacy where an antibiotic prescription awaited us. And now, three days later, a disease that might have killed her two hundred years ago is gone from her body.

We can engineer buildings and cities and transportation systems that connect entire countries and continents. I have a device on the table next to me right now that allows me to send a message to multiple social media networks, FaceTime with my kids, take calls, make a to-do list that will remind me when to do it, and a billion other things, both useful and mundane. I write this sentence on the backlit keyboard of a Macbook Pro that is more powerful and with more memory than the devices they used to put men on the moon. And that was a pretty amazing technological and scientific feat all its own.

I sit here in this coffee shop drinking an Americano made on a sleek stainless steel machine with espresso beans shipped in from Brazil while listening to Oscar Peterson, who died nearly ten years ago, massage my ears with his jazz piano skills. How? How does this compilation of experiences and sensations happen? Man's creativity and ingenuity as they reflect the image of God by doing and making amazing things.

Creativity is art. It is inventiveness and ingenuity. It is the pursuit of beauty and efficiency. It is the connecting of ideas and resources to make new ideas and better resources. You and I were created to create and discover, created for the vocation of reflecting God's image. But we were not created to live in isolation. God made man, and it was, the Bible tells us, not good for him to be alone. He was to be in relationship, to live communally. Our vocation is a collective one, a joining together of individuals into cultures to reflect God.

And as people come together to do this, to find ways for lives to intersect and work together, cultures and subcultures are created. This means that cultures reflect the image of God. In the West we think individualistically—"I am made in God's image." In many parts of the world, though, people view identity as collective—"We are made in God's image." Both are correct so long as they do not discount the other. In many cases, the movement of a culture, a group of people, can actually reflect more of God. Like a mosaic is many bright tiles combined to create a picture, so a culture is many little reflections combined to present a greater image.

When We Broke Creation

Look around the world and something becomes very obvious: we don't do a very good job reflecting God either individually or as cultures. There is a whole lot of awful, a whole lot of pain and misery and ugliness. Culturally it seems that we're headed more toward hell in a hand basket (or on a road paved with good intentions or maybe driving the Highway to Hell while listening to *Hell's Bells*—so many ways to get there) than doing anything especially heavenly, and the same goes for the rest of world. For every great invention or beautiful work of art there is an invention of destruction and a work of chaos or exploitation. Individually we have good days and bad days—days when we represent God well and days we're awful at it.

Something isn't right.

At the very beginning of this chapter I posed the question about how we could keep curiosity from going wrong, but wrong is precisely where it went in the Garden of Eden—for the very first time. God gave Adam and Eve a single command—do not eat from that one tree—for their own good and fullness of life. He was not taking something good from them; He was keeping them from something beyond them. But Satan spun his deceit and told them they would not surely die, told them God must be hiding something delightful behind that command. And curiosity went off the rails. Instead of pursuing truth, instead of living their vocation, Adam and Eve sought knowledge that was not theirs to have and turned the nobility of godly curiosity upside down. They used curiosity for their ends and it became their end.

Adam and Eve broke creation because they stepped outside their vocation. Instead of seeking to *reflect* God, they sought to *be* Him. They sought to promote themselves to the position of giver of vocations instead of doer of them. And every day since then mankind has followed suit. And lest you look back and blame Adam and Eve for your hardships and the pain in the world, you and I very likely would have done the exact same thing. We bear the same limitations in fortitude and the same propensity for succumbing to temptation. We too yearn for knowledge that is not ours to have, knowledge too wonderful for us. What we do wrong today was not just foisted on us. It is part of who we are because they broke creation and we continue in kind.

From that day forward the image bearers of God have reflected poorly. We have echoed dully, like shouting in a carpeted room. We reflect as many ungodly things as we do things of God. We take good things, things God made as beautiful, and skew or pervert them so that He is no longer recognizable through them. That is sin in a nutshell: taking things God intended for good and perverting them to ungodly ends.

We reflect it in our own lives, and culture multiplies and magnifies that. My selfishness combined with yours combined with three hundred million other Americans makes us a nation of self-absorbed gluttons and navel-gazing whiners convinced we are the greatest nation in history and superior to the rest of the world. And that is just one example. Every culture both shapes and increases the sins of its people. But every culture also combines talents and accomplishments to give people a platform to build upon those talents and accomplishments.

Creation is broken, but it is not lost. I am broken but not lost, so are you, and so is every culture across the world. Every person and collection of people have the capacity to beautifully reflect God and echo His voice, but each fails much of the time and in many ways. This world is, once all that is added up, a rather complicated, confusing place.

So, Curiosity?

Where does curiosity fit in all this about truth, creation, vocation, creativity, God's image, sin, cultures, and whatnot? It is the key to sorting it all out, to making a way forward, to actually fulfilling the vocational calling we have to reflect God's image.

We are not only created to reflect and echo God, we are tasked with doing so in all of life. We were created in a manner unlike any other being, able to create. A huge portion of creativity is discovery.

Jonas Salk didn't create the polio vaccine from nothing; he discovered it. Albert Einstein didn't create the theory of relativity from nothing; he discovered it through research and trial and error. Beethoven wrote symphonies, created them, but even those were based on compilations of little discoveries along the way. The same is true for Steve Jobs's inventions, and Winston Churchill's leadership. Creativity is discovery put to good use in a fresh way. We cannot discover unless we ask and search; that is curiosity!

Curiosity killed the cat. —Agent Vega

It also cured polio.[16] —Simon, The Mentalist

Yet, while we are created to reflect God, He never actually discovered anything. He was never curious about anything. He never learned anything. That's one of the effects of knowing everything, being everywhere, and being eternal. He knows the inner workings of every bit of matter, the gravitational relationships between cosmic bodies, the thoughts and emotions of humans and animals alike, the history of everything and how all things came to pass, and what will come to pass in the future. And He understands how all of them fit together all of the time across all eras. He created it all and sustains it all. There is nothing for God to discover.

How can we reflect an eternal, infinite God if He has a nature and characteristics we can never emulate? Vocation. We're back to that word again. A calling, a set of tasks to which we are suited. Our reflection of God is not passive. Our echoing is not inactive. We do not echo like a canyon wall, still and static while noise bounces off of us. We echo like town criers, taking up the message and passing it along clearly and loudly. We reflect on purpose, with intention, by taking action.

And one of those actions is discovery—about God Himself. In order to represent God to the world, we must know Him, and to do that we must learn. We must search for truth about His nature, His character, and His work. We must explore *both* His Word and His world. We absolutely must be curious if we are Christians. Without it we cease to grow and we become incapable of fulfilling our purpose in life.

If we start by growing in this divine curiosity, we will then be prepared to begin exploring this weird, complicated messy world that is full of so much amazing truth and beauty and so many awful lies and horror. In bricklaying, a plumb line is the instrument used to determine whether a wall is perfectly vertical and at the proper ninety-degree angle from the ground. Discovery in and of God gives us a plumb line to measure our discoveries of the world. Are they true? Are they right? Do they reflect God? And, more subtly, what pieces of them are good and what pieces need to be discarded or ignored?

Godly curiosity keeps us from becoming simplistic legalists who just label everything as either good or bad. This is discernment, a trait all wise Christians have, and one that relies on curiosity so that it can deeply understand. Most things in our world are not purely good or bad. Curiosity rooted deeply in God's truth—discernment, that is— helps us see which aspects of culture or creation are beautiful and true and which are not. Being simplistic means we throw a lot of babies out with even more bath water (an absolutely horrific word picture, if you think about it).

To be a vibrant Christian is to be curious. The more we discover of God, the more truth we will know and embody and reflect. The more truth we embody and reflect, the more we will recognize it in other parts of creation—other cultures, unfamiliar circumstances, new relationships, novel inventions. Our knee-jerk reaction as humans is to label all unfamiliar things as "bad" or at least to be skeptical. Godly curiosity balances realistic understanding of the world's sinfulness with a passionate desire to see and find truth, so new things become exciting and full of possibility yet without naïveté or ignorance.

Without curiosity we cannot be what God designed us to be. We cannot know Him or His truth as we ought or care for His creation as He wishes. We cannot understand this world or its Creator or its faults or its blessings. Curiosity is where that all begins, and curiosity must begin at God Himself—searching, asking, digging, discovering, growing. If we start there, His image will reflect and His voice will resonate from us into a world that needs it deeply.

Chapter 3

Where, Oh Where, Have All the Curious People Gone?

"HAVE YOU EVER WONDERED how . . . ?"

"Have you ever wondered why . . . ?"

"Have you ever wondered if . . . ?"

You pose these questions to your friends as you walk down the street or to your spouse as you drive to the kids' track meet. You have a friend who asks them when you sit at the coffee shop or bar or cafeteria or back patio. To the listener they seem to arise from nowhere, a random figment of thought birthed from nowhere and leading to nothing. To the asker, though, they arise from the eyes, the senses, the mind all working in concert unbidden and unceasing. The asker notices something and it reminds her of something that connects to two other thoughts, that harken a memory, and the result is this kind of question.

How? Why? What if? Questions about nature, about history, about people's backstories, about politics, about city layout, about architecture, about music, about possibilities or plans, about *anything*.

Most people are caught off guard, surprised by such questions. They've never considered who might live in that old run-down house or how long it's been there. They don't really care what breed of horse that is or what the demographic makeup of this neighborhood is. They're not that interested in how Santa Claus, Indiana, or Condemned Bar, California, got their names. (Really, these are actual names of actual towns in real places.)

They don't think much about the culture of the immigrants in the apartment complex one block over. They don't consider why the city schools perform dramatically worse than suburban ones or what the effects of gentrification are on those who are priced out of neighborhoods where they grew up. And they don't wonder about the mind-set, the training, the perspective, or the motive of the officers policing their town. In these examples it is easy to see how a lack of curiosity is not just problematic, but tragic.

When cultures and subcultures are separated by a chasm and the lack of understanding is tremendous, tragedy can strike. While a lack of curiosity about many things is relatively benign, in this case it is malignant. It is not merely a lack of interest or understanding; it is the petri dish in which anger, resentment, prejudice, and eventually violence grow.

The fact that it takes four engines to push and pull that freight train doesn't catch their eye, and neither do they wonder what's in the endless crawl of boxcars delaying their arrival at work. If they notice at all that tonight's sunset is shades of violet and yesterday's was soft gold, nothing much registered other than that both were pretty, and "pretty" is not the reaction of the curious. No wondering why.

Most things don't cross most people's minds or spark a question. Most people's minds are stupefied by comfort and overwhelmed by busyness. The structure and pace of life leaves little room or motivation for asking questions or noticing anything new.

Childlike Wonder

I asked a million questions about these types of things when I was a little boy. Most children do. They notice all sorts of stuff and their questions just bubble out. Over the years, though, I learned that asking such questions often draws confused stares or bemused smiles—the kind that made me feel as if I'd said something silly or unintentionally funny. As a child and adolescent, they were more likely to draw mockery because kids hadn't learned to suppress their judgment and express it politely (as confusion or bemusement). Now, as an adult, such questions live mostly in my mind and the minds of other curious people. We know better than to ask. Or at least we fear people's impression of us too much to do so. We simply believe we have too much at stake to risk being thought weird.

It's a delight when I cross paths with someone else who revels in the random. Like C. S. Lewis said in *The Four Loves*: "Friendship . . . is born at the moment when one man says to another 'What! You too? I thought that no one but myself . . .'"[17] Such occurrences are rare. Most people just don't *wonder* all that much, at least not out loud. (Maybe we'd have that "you too?" moment more often if we were bolder to ask our questions instead of think them and if we worried less about being thought an oddball.) Most people don't ask many questions about many things, or even a few things. They don't notice. Things don't strike them. So when curious people actually do ask these seemingly random questions, we draw blank stares or sympathetically confused chuckles.

Just Living Life

> When you lose your curiosity, you basically have started to give up on life.[18] —John Maxwell

Most of us just live our lives. We live by routine and stay in our lane. Our lives carve tracks that we follow day after day, month after month. And for most people that kind of steady consistency is the ideal. Anything outside of that track is an interruption, a nuisance, or even a crisis.

We make decisions based on this narrow track. What do I need to live *my* life better? What will help me be a better employee, parent, student, or spouse? What will simplify and enhance my life? These are our filters. And we ignore all that doesn't fit through the filter. It's not that those other things are necessarily bad. It's that they don't matter. At least to us. These aren't bad questions or filters by which to make decisions. They just aren't the only the questions we should be asking, and they aren't the most important ones.

The result is that we shrink our lives. We shrink them to our own needs (or perceived needs) and preferences and schedules and commitments. We shrink the margins of our life to leave room for a little relaxation, a little personal betterment, a little Netflix (and chill, if we're lucky). We seek to know what we must and little else. We ask those questions that progress us down our track. Really, though, progress is just time passing, and we're just trying not to rock the cart on the way to wherever we're going.

> Knowledge comes by eyes always open and working hands.[19] —Jeremy Taylor

J. R. R. Tolkien, in his classic story *The Hobbit,* describes a race of beings who sound strikingly like us in the Western world. They live simple lives and love their food and drink. They are suspicious of the outside world, even fearful, but are fascinated by tales of it. They love bright colors, dapper dressing, mild scandal, and a comfy home to hide away in. In short they desire simple lives with the right amount of pleasure and the occasional tale of what happens "out there" across the borders of the Shire, their home.

We are real-life hobbits, seeking peaceful lives centered on daily needs, basic comforts, a little gossip, and some good parties. We want to handle our business, do our work, and be compensated fairly for it. But we really want the outside world to stay outside. The outside world doesn't just mean faraway places but simply other people's issues and stories. Those are their problem. Don't invade our Shire. And don't expect me to go on any adventures or quests into the great unknown, especially not with anybody strikingly different than I. I get the adventure I need from watching reality TV, nature documentaries, and listening to missionaries talk about the other side of the world. If I get really adventurous I can go find a video on YouTube of someone doing parkour on the Eiffel Tower or washing windows on the Burge Khalifa.

But then our carefully directed and graded track intersects and merges with another, that of someone whose experiences differ wildly from our own. We can't help it; it's unexpected, an intrusion. A wizard, as it were, knocks on our door, or a pile of dwarves devours everything in our pantry and sings a tale of a dragon. We begin to realize that our shrunken life isn't enough to make sense of their lives and stories. We've heard rumor of such people and such experiences, but they were much more palatable online or "out there" where they belong.

Your brother returned from combat in Afghanistan struggling with PTSD and the loss of his brothers in arms. He tells you there's no way for you to understand or help. Maybe he's right; what can you say? A single mother just moved in next door, and you don't know quite how to connect or relate or help or if you even want to get involved. Your team at work just hired a Chinese-American. You don't want to be insensitive or awkward, so how do you bridge the cultural gap? Is there even a cultural gap? Your cute, bright baby girl turned into a seemingly sullen, angry metal head as a teen. What happened? Is there any chance she'll ever talk to you again?

We don't understand and we don't understand how to understand. We don't know what questions to ask or what resources to use. We have suppressed and excluded curiosity for so long that we no longer have any idea where to find it or how to use it. We are stuck.

Conflict happens. Friction happens. Empathy is nowhere to be found because empathy requires walking a mile in their shoes; but we don't know where to walk or even how, and, frankly, we like our own shoes quite a lot. We are inert, lost, frustrated, and confused.

How did we get here?

We Gave Up before We Started

> I think, at a child's birth, if a mother could ask a fairy godmother to endow it with the most useful gift, that gift would be curiosity.[20] —Eleanor Roosevelt

I have two daughters, ten and seven at the time I write this. Their questions are endless and wildly varied. They notice everything and ask about it. They hear everything and ask about it (an effective, if embarrassing, corrective for me and my mouth). They are vibrant learners, sponges for knowledge. And I didn't teach them to be that way. It's how kids *are*. Every child is, by nature, a questioner, a learner, curious. If they are given a supportive, loving environment, this curiosity flourishes.

Abused and neglected children are unable to express their curiosity; it's been suppressed and they are simply surviving. When every ounce of energy is going to survival—how to avoid the next beating, where the next meal is coming from, will Mom wake up from her high, when will Daddy's next bender be—all the wonderment of curiosity is stifled by the need to just live. It's true for children and adults, individuals and groups of people (think urban poor or manual laborers in third-world countries). But free them from abuse, from poverty, give them support and freedom, and what happens? Curiosity blooms. It is inherent to childhood.

While curiosity is in us from birth, it is not just a trait. It is not like height or hair color or the sound of our voices. Curiosity is a discipline, a habit, a skill set. We know this because we lose it. Every child is curious, some quietly and some boisterously. Some adventurously and some studiously. Some artistically and some athletically.

But by the time they're in high school, curiosity has given way to "learning," the dreaded expectation of school.

Not only that but wondering stops being cool. It's not normal to be a bright-eyed question asker. It's not okay to be overly noticed as a pre-teen and teen, and too many questions get one noticed. Most kids want to stand out without being noticed. (Thus the fact that most kids dress alike, listen to the same music, and style their hair the same way in the effort to differentiate themselves. We did the same when we were teens.) Curiosity gets one noticed. Eagerness shines too bright. Better to play it cool and not ask those questions.

Then off to college they go where they major in a discipline or specific subject so that they can get a job in a specific field. Students who have varied interests are encouraged to pick one and dig in. Focused education is better than well rounded for entering the workforce, they are told. Don't be a generalist. Be a specialist; master something, they are reminded repeatedly. And philosophy or literature or art don't count—liberal arts are nice in concept, this thinking goes, but offer little future direction. Then, once they're in the work force they put that mastery to use, trundling along creating their little track, their safe, small life.

Into this track they bear children who are full of wonder and curiosity. And the cycle begins again.

So it is that we give up on curiosity before we even start. At the time when it most needs fostering and developing, we begin turning kids away from it. During those tender years when insecurity reigns, we hand them off to an education system bound by awful methods.

What School Doesn't Do

> It is a miracle that curiosity survives formal education.[21] —Albert Einstein

> You can teach a student a lesson for a day; but if you can teach him to learn by creating curiosity, he will continue the learning process as long as he lives.[22] —Clay P. Bedford

We live in the most educated time in history. Between public education, the proliferation of information on the Internet, and easy access to books and other publications, people have more collective knowledge than ever. Every child in America can attend school (although a massive disparity exists in the quality of these schools from place to place and along income lines). More people than ever are graduating from high school and college. We are degree-rich yet we are a bored, uncurious bunch. And school isn't really helping.

Our school system is intent on giving our children essential knowledge. The curricula and the methods create effective test-takers and skilled memorizers full of answers and facts. We train children to master a system, or in many cases, to game the system by learning how to excel at exams while retaining as little as possible. It is technique-based learning, not absorption of truth. It is mill work, developing a narrow set of skills with minimal application in the broader world because it does not catalyze creativity or curiosity.

This is not the teachers' fault in the vast majority of cases. Good teachers, and they are legion, love learning as discovery of knowledge, of truth. They love to see the light go on in a student as she begins to understand and get excited about something. They want learning to be fun so students will fall in love with it. These teachers find ways to make it happen in spite of the system. Their efforts are why so many of us remember that one teacher so fondly.

She taught us to love literature. He opened our eyes to how geometry works. She unlocked our love of art. He gave us confidence to take on challenges. It's not because they helped us ace a standardized test; it's because they sparked a love for something in us.

Yet our system is one that directs children toward a narrower and narrower path, intersecting with fewer and fewer new ideas or opportunities to *discover*. We tell them what they must learn to function in the world, but we don't offer them what they need to live vibrantly and interact well with the world and its inhabitants.

I don't have a proposal for how to fix schools. I don't blame teachers or educators. I know many people who teach at different levels, and they express frustration about these same problems. In fact, I am not sure it is just the school system's fault. I think it is a fault of perspective.

As parents *we* are responsible for the education of our children. We outsource the knowledge exchange to schools because they are better equipped than we to teach our children about math, science, social studies, and art. Our problem is that we define education as math, science, social studies, and art. Those are subjects, fields of learning, areas of discovery.

Education, rather, is about perspective much more than it as about mastering subjects. It is our job to imbue our children with the right perspective—perspective on truth, on people, on life, on the world, on cultures. That cannot be outsourced and that is what schools cannot offer—not Christian schools, not public schools, and not home schooling. Each fails in its own way if leaned on as the sole means of education.

> A sense of curiosity is nature's original school of education.[23] —Smiley Blanton

Perspective comes from seeing things differently, from experiencing things widely. Perspective comes from feeding curiosity and giving it a chance to roam and see and feel. And it comes from seeing and experiencing all these things in a context of biblical truth.

Perspective feeds curiosity because it sees life from different sides and from different points of view. Curiosity then feeds perspective because it asks and seeks and explores and finds new points of view and hidden truths. It's like an endless relay race with each one running a leg then handing off the baton to the other. This is education too, and school cannot offer it to our children. We can. We can exemplify it and teach it and take them with us to find it.

If we entrust our children to schools alone, we are setting them up to be warehouses of knowledge with little idea why it matters and what difference it can make in the world. We are not helping them *be* better. We're simply helping them know more, to be masters of the Scantron. But life is not lived by choosing from options A through D and passing a standardized test. Neither is it lived in safe little grooves we've carved for ourselves. So we must seek perspective and the experiences that create it.

The Side Effects of Uncuriosity

Almost every time I watch TV, I see a commercial for medication of some kind—depression, digestive issues, restless leg syndrome.

Medicine ads are on so often I found them annoying until I realized something: they are sneaky funny. I just needed to listen a little more closely. After spending most of the ad touting the benefits of the pill and telling you to ask your doctor about it (because never forget: doctors need our expert help), the ad switches to a person muttering words in triple time. What words? All the ways the medicine can kill you or at least make you miserable.

"If you experience any of the following, please cease taking this medicine and inform a doctor immediately: swelling of the eyes, blood in your urine, heart palpitations, seizures, lumpy growths, brain aneurysms, uncontrollable laughter, suicidal thoughts, incontinence, cankles, boils, blurred vision, hair loss, etc." It's like the ten plagues God sent on Egypt mixed with a Harry Potter spell.

Suppressing curiosity is kind of like the medicine in one of these ads. What can it do for you? It can make life safe and comfortable. It can give you feelings of being in control and help you manage your life. It will allow you to think of yourself especially highly and think very little about other people's discomfort or needs. In short, *uncuriosity* is the perfect medicine for a life of ease!

Now, about those side effects. We'll try to rattle them off fast enough that it doesn't distract from the sales pitch. Try to read this in triple time and at half volume. It'll be easier on you.

Binary Thinking

There are two kinds of people in the world: Those who divide everything into two groups and those who don't. For example, there are two kinds of people in the world: those who are curious and those who aren't.

That is an example of the kind of bogus thinking that is so pervasive. We love to simplify complex issues that have an array of factors into simplistic dichotomies and then pit one side against the other. As I write this, the nation is preparing for a presidential election, and the Republicans and Democrats are pitted against one another in a typically vicious and depressing standoff. By the time you read this book, we will have a new president, yet all of the following issues will be just as hotly disputed.

We are debating whether Muslim refugees should be allowed in the country and whether Hispanic immigrants should be deported. We are debating the best way to respond to a rash of mass shootings. We are debating issues of police brutality and systemic racism. We are debating matters of abortion and the lives of the unborn. We are debating whether the rich should be taxed more or less heavily than the middle classes. And every debate is being crystalized into a one vs. one argument, one side vs. another. It is always either/or.

This happens because so few people have the intentional curiosity to understand the opposing position and to explore what other positions there might be. We create false either/or constructs instead of recognizing the gray, the gradient that actually represents most issues. Instead we get stupid, simplistic thought arguing for extremes instead of reasoned, balanced thought willing to show respect to the persons on the other side. I say persons because binary thinking often makes us forget the human element of argument, the feelings and values and lives of those we oppose.

It takes curiosity to delve into those depths and complexities. We don't have enough.

Missed Connections

Most people in the world are strangers to us. We don't know them. We know nothing about them. We view them as *stranger* than us. Or we don't view them as anything at all because they are nonentities to us. Only curiosity overcomes this.

When we meet someone and are coming from a place of genuine curiosity, no longer do we see them as strange but as a person with a story we do not yet know. We ask questions and find out about them and along the way—there it is—a connection! We find something in common. It might be small like a genre of music we enjoy or a favorite baseball team. It might be significant like graduating from the same college or knowing the same family. The more human and relational the connection the more significant it is. All of a sudden the stranger becomes an acquaintance. And an acquaintance isn't too far from being a friend.

This doesn't mean we must all be extroverted, asking people questions all the time and seeking out strangers to be our new best friend. That is not how God inclined many of us. It just means when we interact with new people, we should see them as *new people* not strangers. It means we take the risk of offending our mothers by ignoring "stranger danger" and we ask questions that help people feel valued and understood. As we learn to see everyone as fellow image bearers, this becomes a natural next step, or maybe a supernatural one. Find that point of connection. Your narrow little track of a life has intersected with theirs. Make something of it. Be curious about them. If you aren't, you have lost an opportunity and so have they. You have robbed two people.

Depleted Friendships

So many of us lack real friends, true friends. In fact we are so lacking we are unfamiliar with what a true friend really is. We think of our golf or drinking or coffee or work or yoga buddies. We think of the parents of our kids' friends, those folks we chat with while the kiddos have a "play date" (what used to more commonly be known as simply "play-ing"). These are our friends. But really they're stuck in limbo between acquaintance and true friend. We know more about them than the new acquaintance but not enough to truly call them "friend." We know some details of their lives and they know some of our lives, but we don't trust them with the sensitive bits.

We don't share with them that our marriage is on the brink of collapse. Instead we keep that inside where it eats us up, corroding the joy of each day, while we put on the happiest front we can. We don't share about the anxiety or depression we battle week in and week out. We never reveal our financial hardships and the weight of debt we're carrying. That would be embarrassing. And we just assume that such issues are unique to us; they couldn't possibly have something to share in return.

This is, in part, because we lack curiosity. Curiosity combined with courage presses in and digs deeper. We found out about their outward life—hobbies, preferences, history. But now we take the risk of finding out about their inner life—hopes, beliefs, passions, dreams, fears. Curiosity takes risks and steps into the unknown. It digs into shadowy places where there might be treasure or where there might be pain. This is the grounds for real friendship. The reality is that people are much more likely to open up to us than we think; we just need to go first. In fact, they've been hungering for someone to connect with as well.

Such curiosity is persistent and consistent. Life always changes and so do the people who live it, so we must constantly be seeking, asking, looking for that new perspective so that we can connect with these friends in the right way at the right time. Just because we made a connection once and had one or two deep conversations doesn't mean that connection will last unless we press on. If we do not muster our courage and marshal our energies to invest with curiosity, we will not have the kinds of friends we truly want and need.

Love Lost

The most important friendship many of us have is that of our spouse. But a spouse is no mere friend, if one can rightly call friends "mere." A spouse is a person to whom we have given our whole selves in a commitment that surpasses all others. We have given our whole selves.

How can such a relationship remain alive and vibrant for a whole lifespan?

Curiosity.

We must be insatiably curious about our spouses in a way we are about nobody else. We learn all there is to know about them and then keep learning because what we learned initially has changed or grown. We seek new ways to express love and surprise them with thoughtfulness. That takes curiosity. We ask and observe and explore. We experiment and test all because we want to love them *best* and we are not there yet.

> We never know whom we marry; we just think we do. Or even if we first marry the right person, just give it a while and he or she will change. For marriage, being [the enormous thing that it is] means we are not the same person after we have entered it. The primary problem is . . . learning how to love and care for the stranger to whom you find yourself married.[24] —Stanley Hauerwas

A marriage without curiosity is a tree without water. It will stand for a while, but after a time its leaves will shrivel and fall, the branches will lose pliability, a strong wind will blow, and branches will snap instead of withstanding. In the end the whole thing will crack and crumble and rot, sometimes with a spectacular crash and other times silently from the inside out. Curiosity is the sap, the lifeblood of the relationship to keep it strong through the years. It is the hope marriages have to keep from becoming boring or stale or dry.

God Is . . . ?

> Until our thoughts of God have found every visible thing and event glorious with his presence, the word of Jesus has not yet fully seized us.[25] —Dallas Willard

Our most important human relationships—friend, family, or spouse—pale in comparison to the importance of our relationship with God. How many of us, though, can rightly say we have a *relationship* with God? We have an understanding of Him to some degree. We have collected some knowledge, maybe much knowledge, of Him. Many of us have an acquaintance with God or even the pseudo-friendship of the work buddy or play date parent. We spend a little time and chat some. We like Him well enough so we make it a point to get Him on the calendar every few weeks as time allows. But there are unexplored depths we have never approached.

Last chapter I wrote about the infinity of God and the profundity of His character and nature. Do we have a relationship with *that*? Even if the answer is yes, the answer is not a total yes because there will always be aspects we have yet to discover or understand.

Curiosity drives us to seek the deep truths of God. It leads us to discover aspects of His character and truths of His Word that hide behind a veil or aren't readily visible in the mundane life. It overcomes the preconceptions we have of God that often make us like Him less, often from a legalistic background: God as boss, God as judge, God as distant, God as joyless, God as killjoy, God as impersonal, God as boring, God as powerless, God as puppet master. Curiosity enlarges God in our minds, or rather helps us see His largeness and His largesse, His closeness and His love, His plan and His promise.

Without the desire to see and understand and experience—without curiosity—we are content with a God-loves-me-so-I'm-all-good "relationship." That is barely a relationship at all. That's mild appreciation to a benefactor. It's heartless and moves us not at all. It is lifeless and stagnant. Then again, so is all of life without curiosity.

I Don't Care

> Little minds are interested in the extra-ordinary; great minds in the commonplace.[26]
> —Elbert Hubbard

When we lack curiosity, our world shrinks to the size of our waking hours. What am I doing? What affects me? What do I want? What do I need?

No thoughts of anyone else. No thoughts of anything bigger than ourselves. That's because without curiosity nothing *is* bigger than ourselves. We are our sole point of reference for everything. It's not just that we don't care about other people or their problems; it's that we can't. We can't see past our own lives.

Curiosity enlarges the world. It opens our eyes to the experiences of others, to celebrate or to mourn. It moves us to think about what someone else needs or might like instead of only what we need or want. It shows us that others see things differently and live vastly different lives. Curiosity builds empathy instead of apathy and antipathy. It makes us care about things that we did not and could not.

Better Medicine

> I think the key to the future is curiosity. I look at the people I admire most and they're curious people, they're open, they're interested, they haven't arrived.[27] —Carey Nieuwhof

If Uncuriosity is a medicine that promises safety and security, along with all the above side effects—what might the medicine called Curiosity offer?

To begin with, it makes no false promises or claims of comfort. Curiosity often leads people into uncomfortable situations or realizations, but it's the kind of discomfort that comes with stretching and expanding and growing—the pain after a good workout, the mental fatigue of wrestling through a tough text, the nervous anticipation of going on a first date. Or maybe it is not something so pleasant—the internal peace of knowing you acted with conviction even at your own expense (job loss, broken relationship, financial hardship) or that you showed kindness when it wasn't deserved or reciprocated.

Curiosity isn't a quick fix. It is more like a diet or a lifestyle. It demands work and a plan and consistency. It requires fostering because, if we don't, it dissipates quickly and we find ourselves back on the Uncurious pill. We'll look at some of the ways we can foster curiosity later in the book. Right now let's look at the benefits of it. In many ways they are the opposite of the side effects of Uncuriosity, but they are more than that as well.

Cumulative

The most significant benefit of curiosity is its cumulative effect. Uncuriosity is inherently small and stays small. It isolates every person.

The only cumulative effect is that everyone cares nothing about others. Curiosity is just the opposite. It builds on itself. It enlarges individual lives and connects them to others, which then enlarge each other's lives.

Brian Grazer is a renowned movie producer who runs Imagine Entertainment along with Ron Howard. Grazer and Howard have partnered to make some of the most successful and critically acclaimed movies and TV shows in the past three decades (*Apollo 13, A Beautiful Mind, Parenthood, 24, Friday Night Lights*). That is enough for most people to find Grazer an interesting and compelling person, but what captured my attention was his intentional habit of "curiosity conversations." Starting when he was in early twenties and just trying to break into the movie industry, Grazer intentionally sought out people he thought might be interesting and asked them questions for no other reason than to hear their stories, perspectives, and to learn from them. Early on he had to connive his way into the offices of high-powered people, but in the years since he has been able to sit down with presidents, scientists, inventors, even Fidel Castro.

The impact of these conversations, Grazer explains in his book *A Curious Mind*, is not a list of lessons or collection of knowledge. It is the cumulative impact of varying perspectives and the thoughts of bright people. He writes about how it has impacted his movie making and which movies get made and how it has shaped him as a boss. Grazer could go into these conversations looking for something particular—a movie idea, a specific piece of wisdom—but by just listening and absorbing he has found the conversations to have a much more comprehensive effect on his life and work. And Grazer's work has impacted millions of people in one way or another.

Curiosity has a sort of a pay-it-forward aspect because every time a curious person asks a question it has the potential to spark curiosity in someone else too. Curiosity pushes people to do more, think more, be more, and as more people live expanded lives they are bound to overlap and intersect. When this happens, each person's life changes again and more opportunities are provided for discovery and new experiences. Curiosity is exponential, not isolated.

Self

While curiosity is not isolated, it starts with the individual—with you and me. We begin to see more, ask more, explore more, wonder more, discover more. As we do, our minds and hearts are expanded. Our intellects are sharpened as we encounter new ideas and ways of thinking. Our character is honed as we learn to see through new eyes and feel what others are feeling—what is commonly called empathy and emotional intelligence. Our skills are enhanced as we observe how others excel at their work or craft. Curiosity becomes exponential in us. As we develop it creates a desire to develop it more. Learning and experience begets learning and experience. What we become is a more vibrant, interesting, interested, caring, connected person able to do and be far more than when we languished as uncurious.

Relationships

As we grow in vibrancy and capacity to care, we find ourselves with the potential to have relationships with people we never would have dreamed. I have a friend who intentionally rented an apartment in a neighborhood of Nashville home to Turkish immigrants because he wanted to know them and serve them well, to befriend them. I have another friend who is Caucasian who lives in a neighborhood on the south side of Chicago that is almost entirely African-American because he believed that if he and his family were to serve the community well, they had to be neighbors and share life. The ministry he leads is making a dynamic difference in their neighborhood through job creation, a small business incubator, technology training, and sharing the gospel. I know dozens of families who have adopted children from all over the world to give them a *family*, the closest and most meaningful of relationships. This isn't outreach or charity; it is relational love overcoming cultural differences.

Curiosity not only expands the playing field; it changes the rules of the game altogether. Social norms, long-held stereotypes, systemic challenges, and cultural differences are no longer the obstacles they once were, but rather the acknowledged starting points to conversation and understanding. Consistent curiosity leads, over time, to understanding the core of those we once perceived as vastly different from us.

Church

Think about your church or the church you grew up in. Now imagine if that church was full of truly curious people. What might be different?

Likely the church would be a more caring place, deeply aware of people's needs and challenges. It would be a safe place for those struggling because people would take the time and ask the questions to understand their difficulties. Tension and infighting would diminish because people would be curious enough to learn what others really said and really meant instead of construing meaning and creating drama or conflict. It would move toward being more diverse racially, socioeconomically, and educationally because people would be deeply interested in those different from themselves instead of frightened of them or intimidated by them. And more than anything it would be a church full of people in rich relationship with God because they would be searching and asking and looking for what more there is about His character and person and work and word.

A curious Bible study will dig deeper, ask more pointed questions, and apply truth more intentionally. A curious counseling ministry will dig deep into the pains and struggles of hurting people. It will not find the simplest solution but rather search for the best one. A curious small group ministry will not just pattern groups the way they have always been done but rather seek to learn what style works best for this church's culture and demographics. It will seek out the best leaders, not just the available ones. A curious outreach ministry will determine efforts by culture and need, not calendar and tradition. It will find new ways to partner with the community institutions—schools, police, Boys & Girls Clubs, other churches. And a curious church will constantly evaluate its efforts to see if they are making a difference. Are lives being changed? Are needs being met? Are people meeting Jesus and growing in their relationship with Him?

Neighborhoods, Communities, and Society

A church like this one could transform a neighborhood. Each Sunday its attendees would gather, worship, and connect, then flood outward into their homes and jobs and lives and take that impact with them. People would want to visit a church like that because it cares and shows them something of God's love and nature they have never seen. Individual people will connect with neighbors and coworkers, and those people will see something of Jesus in their lives in how they ask and learn and care. People might begin to see Christianity as a belief system that changes lives and loves deeply because it clings to a God who changes lives and loves deeply.

Throughout a community, needs will be met because people in the church know about them and know that they are part of a collection of people who can help. A curious church is aware of who in its midst has needs and who can meet which needs. Church members will be able to tell people of Jesus and His gospel in a manner that connects because they will know the mental state, the circumstances, and the background story of the person with whom they are conversing. Over time a church full of curious people can root itself deep in a community as a need-meeting, people-loving, Jesus-representing entity that reflects the community it loves so much.

Not by Curiosity Alone

Curiosity is a powerful force, the key to solving many an enigma and overcoming many a challenge. It can genuinely change lives for the better and even change communities and cultures.

But it can do none of these things on its own. Just like any worthwhile pursuit, curiosity can be turned to selfish ends, the furthering of sinful agendas, or the bettering of one person at the expense of another. It can be driven by pride, and the collection of knowledge can fuel that pride. Curiosity is a gift from God but, as Genesis 3 showed us, even good gifts from God can be twisted to evil.

Curiosity is a force for good, for changing lives, when it is driven and shaped and directed by the pursuit of truth like we explored last chapter. But how can we be sure that our motives in curiosity are right? How can we be sure that our pursuit of it is not self-serving? How can we know that we are doing good?

The answer is in Galatians 5:22–23: "But the fruit of the Spirit is love, joy, peace, patience, kindness, goodness, faith, gentleness, self-control." These are the marks of one whose life is in Christ, the Word made flesh, truth embodied. Followers of Christ who are seeking to live a life that honors Him and exemplifies Him will exude these characteristics. They are the standards to which we can hold our curiosity, our hearts, our motives, our actions.

Love: Loving curiosity seeks the good of others. It explores how best to love them, to show love, to express it, to care for them.

Joy: Curiosity is discovery of God's world, His people, His creation, His Word. It ought to be an enthralling, enlivening venture. If curiosity is not increasing our joy and capacity for enjoyment, then something is amiss.

Peace: How can we know the way to peace but through curiosity, through exploring solutions to problems, through seeking the best option? "If possible, on your part, live at peace with everyone" (Rom. 12:18).

Patience: What if there is hope? What if the sun will rise again tomorrow on a new day with new mercies? What if God's promises are really worth trusting in and holding to? These are the questions we must ask while living patiently. They require tenacious, tough, firm, desperate curiosity.

Kindness: What does that person need right now? What would brighten their day? How can I help? Curiosity observes needs and moods and emotions, and kindness seeks to meet those needs and lift spirits.

Goodness: Goodness equates to character. Character is doing what is right whether or not anyone is looking and whether or not the choice is difficult. Curiosity has deeply explored God's Word to learn what it is He expects of us in these difficult and tempting spots.

Faithfulness: To be faithful is to hold fast (patience) and to avoid or defeat temptation. Curiosity is that which helps us learn our proclivities for sin, those temptations to be avoided. It is also that which arms us with God's truth. Curiosity provides a reserve of promises so that when we feel like giving up, we can find the hope to keep plugging, keep fighting, keep fleeing.

Gentleness: Think of how Jesus welcomed the children or responded to the woman caught in adultery or the woman at the well—profound gentleness. He asked questions. He welcomed. He looked beyond the mistakes and into the heart. They felt safe with Him. Our curiosity must be marked by this tone and be driven by these images of Christ.

Self-Control: We are sinful beings, prone to a million failures. We lean toward pride, lust, anger, fear, greed, and gluttony. Our curiosity can fuel every sin as easily as it can be marked by and pursue truth. It is self-control that hits the brakes before we begin exploring the sordid, or willfully turns away from the lurid. Self-control sets the needful boundaries on our consumption and aims our expressions. Without it we can become horrid quickly.

These marks are inward and outward. They are personal and communal. They are a metric of godliness, a measure of whether we have gone astray or are pursuing holy curiosity. The great thing is that if our curiosity is aimed the right way, it will help us grow in the Spirit—curiosity is exponential. If our curiosity has gone astray, humbly gauging it against these markers will show us where our error is so we can repent and recalibrate and make right any wrongs.

Start Now

Some who read this will see themselves in these pages as a curious person, itching to learn and know and grow. To you I say keep going. Hone your curiosity. Aim it. Use it. Develop it for good to make a difference instead of simply collecting knowledge. Love others better. Connect with new people. Impact your neighbors and your community. You are on the right track.

Others of you will feel a twinge of something, memory maybe, nostalgia about when you used to be curious, when you used to create and ask and explore. But that was a long time ago in a bygone era before the concerns and responsibilities of life took over. Your life is locked in now, it has its course and you live in it. To you I ask, why? Why can't things change? How might becoming more curious enhance your life and the lives of those around you? Aren't there some simple, accessible ways you could begin?

Start with a single curious question. Just pick one.

"What if . . . ?"

"How does . . . ?"

"Who do I know that . . . ?"

Then aim that question at your close circle, the life you already lead and see where it takes you. More questions will follow, but you don't start big.

The next several chapters will explore how curiosity affects specific areas of life. Maybe these will inspire you or give a sense of where to start. At the very end of the book there is a section of specific steps you can take to live a more curious life, but I think you should read that last, after seeing what a difference curiosity can make in life, society, and faith.

Part 2

Curious About . . . ?

Chapter 4
The Right Stuff

He who can no longer pause to wonder and stand rapt in awe, is as good as dead; his eyes are closed.[28] —Albert Einstein

Be curious. Read widely. Try new things. What people call intelligence just boils down to curiosity.[29] —Aaron Swartz

I LOVE SPORTS, AND, sadly, have a deep affinity for the teams from Minnesota—Timberwolves, Vikings, Twins, Gophers football and basketball. I say "sadly" because if you are at all familiar with sports, you know that Minnesota rivals only Cleveland in its rare ability to offer new hope each season and then crush the souls of fans in cruel and unusual ways. When I was in early elementary school, my older brother bequeathed to me his collection of baseball cards, mostly 1980s Topps. I spent hours poring over them, arranging them, studying them, and trading them with friends. In those early days an affinity was born in me for sports statistics and sports trivia. To this day my mind is full of Kirby Puckett's 1986 season stats, Kevin Garnett's quiet but promising 1995 rookie season, and Randy Moss's breakout for the Vikings in 1998.

All useless knowledge, right? What good does it do me to know that Sam Mitchell is the second leading scorer in Timberwolves history? Wouldn't I be better off devoting that brain space, that energy to studying something more worthwhile? Maybe, but rather than digging into my propensity for pointless trivia, I think we should look at the very question itself.

Would I be better off if . . . ?

Isn't there something more worthwhile?

Most of us tacitly assume that some knowledge is more valuable than other knowledge. If we hear that someone is going to school to study Renaissance literature, we start making "Well, I hear the shoe sales business is booming" jokes. But if we hear that someone is going to study business or medicine we nod approvingly. "Excellent choice, lots of possibilities there."

Areas of knowledge hold a place in our mental hierarchy, even if we don't realize it. Business, leadership, productivity, finance, science, medicine, technical skills, and technology fall into one category. Philosophy, history, sociology, anthropology, and maybe literature take up another. Relationships, emotional intelligence, and other people skills—soft skills—have their place too. Theology, well, that's a confusing one because we aren't really sure what to do with it, but we know it has some greater inherent value. Or does it?

What We Value

This all depends on what determines our value system for knowledge. The hierarchy most of us have, at least in the Western world, is highly pragmatic. We value knowledge based on what it will enable us to do. And by "do," I mean, "earn." How will that knowledge secure my future financially? What career doors will it open? If we can draw a direct line from learning to earning, it's valuable to study.

Christians should hold a different value system. We know that we are to love the Lord our God with all our hearts, souls, and minds (minds = knowledge) and love our neighbors as ourselves. So that means we need to invest our minds in something bigger. Maybe this is where theology fits in along with all the other "ologies." But we still fall prey to the cultural value system that says knowledge is only as valuable as what it will gain you. We still look for the earning angle, the pragmatic angle.

As a result we usually separate and compartmentalize our learning. We have the work mind and the spiritual/relational mind. This allows us to spend time digging deep into areas of knowledge we can't quite reconcile.

In the morning we study Scripture, and at night we read a Christian living or personal growth book (kind of like this one?). Or maybe nighttime is for reading a great novel or watching Netflix's latest great show. We bookend our day with the things that aren't as much skill based as they are good for our hearts—and this is only if we're actually doing well. Many of us struggle to feed our souls either time of day or anywhere in between.

In between those bookends we are workers—skills, leadership, study, creativity, learning, productivity. We are locked in on our work and those skills that make a living. We soak up those bits of learning that enhance our ability to *do*.

This dichotomy allows us to do what we know we ought and to do what culture tells us we ought. How do the two relate? Does one enhance the other or are they in conflict? Probably best not to ask. Just keep doing both and doing your best. At least that's how we go through life.

The way we partition our lives indicates just how we really value knowledge of different kinds. The spiritual and personal are relegated to the fringes of our energy and time. Our spiritual, emotional, relational, and soul development is not where our energy and devotion truly lies. If you, like me, read this and think, "that's not fair" because you really do care about your soul and your relationships and what you consume for personal investment, then ask yourself what alternative there might be. Is there a better way to work this out?

I suspect most professing Christians are dissatisfied with their spiritual life, their personal life, and their work life in some way. And I think this is because we have neatly divided and ranked them rather than figuring out how to weave them together. What if the ways we think about different areas of learning, about work versus personal life, and about spiritual growth aren't the best ways? What if our rankings of knowledge are wrong? What if the very structure I used to divide the investment—morning and evening, segmented hours—is inadequate and actually reflects the binary thinking of the uncurious? "These hours are designated spiritual hours. These hours are designated productive hours."

Such questions are ones a curious person asks. Is this the best way, the right way? Might our efforts to grow personally, to engage wonderful stories, to learn more of God somehow inform and shape our concrete knowledge of work? Might we ask questions that bridge this gap in a nonbinary, curious way? We can start with one concise question.

The Question We Must Answer

So what?

So what if we know lots of stuff about lots of stuff? So what if we are experts at an occupation? So what if we've collected lots of trivia or memorized hundreds of Scripture passages? So what if we read fifty or a hundred books per year? So what if we've visited dozens of countries and seen the world?

In other words, what difference does it make? What can we do with it? How does it change our life or shape our existence or values? How does it drive us deeper into relationship with God, with others, and with our world? And not just do, but be—what does our knowledge and learning turn us into? How is it shaping us?

Some knowledge is actionable, but all worthwhile knowledge should be formative in some way. It forms our intellect, our mood, our souls, our faith, our outlook, our awareness of the world. It changes the formula, the mixture, that makes up our being just a little bit.

No knowledge matters if we cannot answer this simple question about it. *So what?* A simple question, yes, but not easy to answer.

Collecting knowledge is like building a library in your mind. You find a volume here, a tome there, a pamphlet somewhere else. You complete some sets and have scattered materials on other subjects. Over time it becomes an impressive collection. You can dip into it when a question arises. But what good is it if it is simply collected? Who is it benefitting? How is it benefitting you? A library that is unused is simply shelf upon shelf of wasted paper, and our unexercised knowledge is no better.

I hope to, through the rest of this book, help you see what "so what?" can look like. It's a simple question, but the answer can take a million shapes, and it should. We cannot answer only in simplistic, straight-line ways but instead should look for how one answer leads to another, to another and so on. We should begin to see how our spiritual knowledge informs, how our relational knowledge informs, how our cultural knowledge informs, how our vocational knowledge informs, and other ways too.

Knowledge is as good as what we can do with it and what it does to us. This means that, yes, some bits of knowledge are more valuable than others. (Sorry Kirby, Kevin, and Randy.) But it also means that as we grow in active curiosity, we'll be surprised at the fruit some seemingly innocuous bit of knowledge can bear. The more times we see this the more we will be on active lookout for things we can learn that might be nothing or might be really something—something transformative for us or someone else.

David Letterman used to have a recurring bit on *The Late Show* when he hosted called "Is This Anything" where they would feature a person or group doing, well, stuff—it could be juggling, could be hula hooping, could be unicycling, could be all of the above at the same time. After a few seconds of watching these people or groups, Letterman and his sidekick, Paul Schaeffer, would chat briefly to determine whether what they just saw was "anything." It was an amusing bit for its absurdity and brevity, and that's representative of how we often feel in sorting through knowledge. There are piles of the seemingly mundane and we have to determine whether or not it is anything. Is it worthwhile, worth remembering, worth considering? Some knowledge, we will determine, is something. Some knowledge is decidedly not anything.

Over time we will become more active curators of our knowledge. A curator is the person who not only organizes and keeps record of a collection but also sees where the gaps are and looks for new items to fill them. And that's precisely what we will learn to do—see the gaps and fill them, learn what is valuable and how to care for it. But we will not stop at effective curation, not if we are truly curious and not if we truly care about the "so what?" We will learn how to find the knowledge we need when we need it and do with it what we can to build our faith, our relationships, and our world.

Putting Knowledge to Use

Knowledge is worth as much as what you do with it or how it shapes you. If you have profound knowledge of life-altering genetic research and do nothing with it, then it is worth less than if I use my sports trivia knowledge to spark a new friendship. If you've graduated from seminary and are well-versed in theology, it means nothing unless it is expanding your heart for Jesus and for those who still need Him.

This doesn't mean we must be using all knowledge all the time. That is impossible for anyone except God. But it means that as we learn we must be looking for any and all connections between our new knowledge and something useful. It means we must be letting knowledge find the cracks in our soul to seal them and we must let new knowledge raise the level of our thinking and our worship. It means we must have an imagination that says, "This could come in really handy someday."

If this were physical stuff we were collecting, people would call us pack rats, with a shed and a garage full of tools, parts, knickknacks, and various odds and ends. But we need to be able to see a truth and think of all the ways it might be useful—useful to connect to another person, useful to teach a child, useful to reveal something of God, useful to bring a smile to someone's face, useful to help someone in need, useful to create something beautiful, useful to protect or defend truth. And this imagination, this curiosity, is what allows us to *do* with our knowledge.

Think of those people who do the most formative and inspirational work—teachers, artists, entrepreneurs, missionaries, ministers, social workers, and those creative people who are always finding new and better ways to do things. What do they have in common? They take their knowledge, be it big or small, be it varied or narrow, and they make something of it. It shapes and motivates them; they *must* share and make and create and tell. It defines them. They connect with other knowledge and other people to create a better world. They don't live in the rut of "just living life." They ask questions until they discover how what they have, what they know can merge with what others have and know to make a new experience and life. They are *curious* and want to connect their little bit of knowledge with the great big world God has created. And in so doing they bring something new and better to the world.

Thomas Edison was credited as saying, "To invent you need a good imagination and a pile of junk." Well, we have our pile of junk—all this knowledge. Do we have the imagination to begin inventing? Will we ask the necessary questions and push the boundaries of our present rut to begin doing something with the knowledge we have?

Good Knowledge

One pressing question remains, one that I alluded to but never answered: is all knowledge created equal?

Earlier in this chapter we saw that we tend to partition knowledge into private and public, work and personal, sacred and secular. We create a false dichotomy based on a false sense of value—learning should lead to earning. We define and organize knowledge in markedly uncurious ways by deciding it must be one or the other (Binary Thinking Alert).

On the other hand there's the value system many Christians have, especially ministry-minded ones: spiritual and theological learning is more valuable than other learning. I grew up in the church as a pastor's kid. I was steeped in biblical teaching and theological basics. I went on to study theology in college, and for a long time had a sense of superiority toward those who studied "lesser" subjects like literature, business, or communications. Of course if I had actually absorbed the truth of Christian theology, I would have realized two important things. First, if you're a follower of Jesus, there's no place for a sense of superiority.

Second, theology proper is not inherently more valuable than any other area of learning. Like all learning, it is as valuable as the impact it has on our being and decisions in our vocation of reflecting God to the world.

In fact, these hierarchies—learning is best and theology is best—conflict with each other because they both claim superiority. And neither leaves room for valuing the arts or the humanities much at all. And then there's the problem that this entire argument is inhuman, disconnected from the realities of people's lives. In determining which knowledge is the most valuable, we must follow our own advice and ask, "So what?"

So what if we know a lot about a lot?

- Does it show us more of God and draw us closer to Him?
- Does it connect us with other people and their cultures and their needs?
- Does it help us understand and serve our world better?
- Does anything we have learned help us create better goods that reflect God's creativity in us?
- Are we able to teach truth more effectively to more people?
- Are we able to delineate truth from lies better based on what we know?

Such standards determine whether knowledge is valuable and worth pursuing and collecting, and based on them *nothing* is trite.

God made you and me and everyone else with unique passions and gifts. Since none of us can adequately reflect God's image, He made us varied and different. Look around; look at the incredible variety of people; each one reflects a small and invaluable bit of who God is. Each of us uniquely reflects and expresses God's image, and our respective relationship with God and His creation will show different facets of

His truth to the world. That means that my love for sports is a means through which I can reflect something of God to the world. And the same is true for your love of jazz, movies, historical fiction, dance, or whatever it is. If you see God's reflection and truth in something, it is no longer trite; it is a connection point to glory.

Our aim must be to connect people and cultures to God's truth so they too can see God's glory. Many people find this truth through explicit expressions such as sermons and books. Others, though, find it initially through the care of a neighbor who makes a small connection through mutual enjoyment of baking or barbecuing or baseball or blues music. These same neighbors likely would have turned tail and run if you had sermonized them.

Our knowledge is as trite or meaningful as what we do with it for the love of others and God's glory. If you have the imagination to see connections with things you know and you enjoy and helping others see God's truth, then that knowledge has the potential to be profoundly good. Once we see things this way we'll find profound freedom to be curious. No longer is it a waste of time. Instead it is taking advantage of every movie, every conversation, every book, every everything to see how it might be something worth curating to connect people to the truth that saves.

Real curiosity is not frivolous. It is not the itch that can't be scratched and neither is it the flaky pursuit of a directionless person. Curiosity is the fuel that drives the best leaders, evangelists, parents, spouses, employees, ministers, artists, and friends. It is a hunger to know more truth, so that we can show people more truth, so that our world will see more of God. Curiosity takes the mundanity out of the mundane and breathes life into the most intellectual of pursuits.

In the chapters that follow we will explore how curiosity can shape and drive us in different areas of life. We will see just how much curiosity can help us have a more significant relationship with God, people, and the world around us.

Chapter 5

In-Bounds and Out-of-Bounds

I DID NOT GROW up in a home that banned certain kinds of books or music. We didn't have hard and fast rules about seeing films based on their ratings. Neither were we told that certain areas of interest were a waste of time while others were more valuable, with the exception of Scripture and theology. That was always upheld as the greatest pursuit, a pursuit on a different tier of importance.

In the last chapter I addressed the idea that some knowledge is more significant than other kinds of knowledge. The conclusion I came to is that knowledge is only as valuable as what you do with it and what it does to you.

Because of the weight of theological knowledge, the eternal implications, this conclusion is exponentially true. Knowing Scripture should shape and influence and drive how we pursue all other areas of learning and curiosity. It should serve as the foundation on which our lives are built relationally, vocationally, and intellectually.

It is a sad, even sinful, thing to waste knowledge of any kind, but it is infinitely more sad and sinful to collect knowledge of the living

God and for it to have no impact on us. For this reason I am thankful for the emphasis put on learning and living the truth of God's Word in my home growing up. Over the years I did have to develop in my thinking about the sacred/secular divide and how that mind-set leads to arrogance and disdain for culture and many fields of learning. I did have to learn the significance of "all truth is God's truth." I did have to learn how the truths of Scripture, God's revelation of Himself, rule over but also complement all other areas of learning. But I would have had a much harder time doing this if I had not started with a deep respect and reverence for Scripture taught to me by my parents.

Instead of drawing hard lines and banning things (aside from the most egregious and profane), my parents instead prodded me to think about why I wanted to engage different kinds of entertainment or subject. Instead of saying "no," they asked "why?" Why do you want to see that movie? Why do you think that music is so great? Why do you enjoy that series of novels so much?

I remember reading the *Goosebumps* books in elementary school; those ghoulish horror stories were just scary enough to give a child nightmares, but not so bad as to cause psychological damage. My parents didn't love that I read these, but rather than forbidding me, which would have led me to dig in and fight them, they simply asked what it was that I enjoyed about the stories. They nudged me to consider if there was anything worthwhile about them, and not long after I quit reading them. It wasn't a stroke of conscience or guilty feelings. I simply came to see what my parents were hoping I'd see: there are many better stories to be reading that offer much better payoff, so why not try them?

When I was in high school I was planning to go see *Saving Private Ryan*. My dad didn't know a lot about it other than the fact that it had the reputation as an incredibly intense, gory movie due to its realistic depiction of World War II's storming of Omaha Beach during the invasion of Normandy. He wasn't sure why his teenage son wanted to revel in such a scene, so he asked some questions.

Again, he didn't forbid. He didn't fight. He just checked motives and asked about other content in the movie that might be questionable.

I'd done my homework. He listened to my answers. I went on my way and watched the movie, and am so glad I did. Brutal as it is, *Saving Private Ryan* is powerful. If my dad had drawn a hard line based on a rating or a reputation instead of asking questions, I would have missed out and likely resented him too.

My parents' questions served as filters—filters for quality and morality. They taught me to be active in my engagement with culture instead of passively absorbing it. And, maybe most importantly, they allowed and encouraged me to explore numerous areas of interest because I knew I wouldn't be stonewalled if I was curious.

Added to this was their own curiosity, especially my mother's. She was an avid reader and read to my siblings and me from infancy on. She read stories of adventure and war and love and courage and history. Stories opened a world to me. (They also taught me cool things like what being drawn and quartered means and what it's like to have a barbed arrow removed from your thigh.)

Mom listened to Public Radio and audio books, so I got to hear snippets of hundreds of interviews, news stories, public interest stories, and biographies. She asked us questions and answered questions. When I homeschooled for a couple of years in elementary school, her idea of a field trip was a train trip from Atlanta to Washington, D.C., with stops at dozens of battlefields and monuments along the way culminating with tours of the various Smithsonian museums, the capitol building, and the White House. The seeds of curiosity were planted and watered and that garden was well tended.

No subject was out of bounds for me. I had my specific interests, but I knew that I could go find answers to any question about any subject. And, as curiosity always does, those questions begat more questions. Curiosity led to more curiosity. And that has not ceased.

A Key Question

One of the most important questions to curiosity is, "What don't I know?" Before we go digging into different subjects, we should explore this, yet it's one of the hardest to answer because, well, we don't know. But we need to know what we don't know.

The limits of your knowledge can't be measured all at once, but as we ask questions and explore our world we will begin discovering more and more pockets of knowledge and experience about which we know nothing. To a curious person that's like a squirrel finding a stash of acorns.

If all this seems big and overwhelming, that's because it is. This world is big and overwhelming. Culture is too. And media, art, and nature. We could spend a lifetime exploring tiny portions of each and not learn the majority of what there is to know about it. And for some that's where curiosity will take them—a deep dig into a single subject or discipline. All this should motivate you! For the rest of your life there will be new things to learn and wonders to behold! Life never needs to be boring.

Where do you start? Start with your life, your work, your neighborhood, your church, your friends, your family, your bookshelves. Ask "What don't I know?" but then ask "What *do* I know?" Find those things that interest you and get you excited or that you've always wondered about and follow that thread. Ask "What else?" because there will be an "else" and it will take you to surprising places. Constantly ask yourself what you see of God in it followed closely by what you're learning about people.

With this as a starting point and a mind-set, let's look at different areas of life and curiosity. Some of these have been cast as trite or shallow or meaningless. Others are so commonplace or seemingly mundane that you may not have given them much thought. My hope is to show how to think meaningfully about "trite" things and show the significance of the mundane.

Society and Culture

> I learn from as many people all the time, anywhere, as I can.[30] —Craig Groeschel

Culture is ubiquitous. We are all part of one, or maybe more than one. Our cultures have subcultures that are only slightly more recognizable. We are to our respective cultures as a fish is to water—the only time we notice it is when we leave it. This means that culture lies largely unrecognized, but it also means that it is one of the greatest opportunities for the curious.

Our natural tendency is to think of ourselves as normal and those who are unlike us as abnormal. We gravitate toward an "us and them" mentality. We associate easily with those most like us in race, class, education, interests, and everything else. The danger of this mind-set is that "we" always end up holding the highest position and value while "they" are lower and lesser, no matter who they may be.

This is why it's vital to be able to see our own cultures from other perspectives, and only curiosity can help us do this. Without curiosity we become prejudiced and on a trajectory toward bigotry. We judge those with different skin or different accents, those from faraway places, those with more or less education and more or less money. We judge from feelings of superiority or feelings of inferiority, either to stay on top or get on top. We don't know much about "them" except that they aren't as good as "us" and we don't like them. Oh yeah, and they talk and smell funny too.

That bigoted view is based on not knowing. We don't know why "they" are the way they are, what they value, their cultural distinctives. We only see differences and miss all commonality and beauty and strength. And we don't really care to know. It's easier not to.

Curiosity says otherwise.

Curiosity knows it doesn't know even if it doesn't know *what* it doesn't know, and it sets out to learn. Instead of seeing other cultures as weird, curiosity sees them as unique. Instead of making assumptions, it asks questions. And it turns those same questions inward, toward its own culture. Why do we do things this way? Why do we believe these things? Why do we treat people this way? What do we excel at? What are we bad at? What is our history? How did we get here? Such questions pointed inward will humble us because they expose our flaws and encourage us because they reveal our strengths. Such questions pointed outward will humble us because they expose strengths in others we never expected and will encourage us because they make relational connections we didn't know could exist.

Curiosity in action will lead us to ask questions of those we perceive to be different that allow them to speak for themselves and express the beauty and strength of their cultures or subcultures. It will open our eyes to God's creative hand and how aspects of His character are expressed in ways our culture misses.

In some ways it is easier to learn to value other cultures than it is to rightly value our own. It is easier to see the good in another culture than to see the flaws in our own. We grade ourselves on a curve and let a lot of "little" stuff go. But find the flaws we must and then grade them rigorously, and once they're graded we must work to correct them. We must pop our own cultural ego bubble.

People are sinners, but so are cultures. Many Christians are willing to address personal responsibility and guilt. We confess our sins and repent. But when it comes to besetting cultural sins, we either deny them or shrug helplessly.

One significant example looms. In the past couple years, with the very public deaths of Trayvon Martin, Mike Brown, Tamir Rice, Walter Scott, Freddie Gray (among others), our country and the church has been confronted with the uncomfortable issue of systemic racism. Minorities, specifically black people in these instances, point to the recurring issues of police violence against black men and boys. They point out the historic pattern of such violence as well as other injustices against the African-American community—employment discrimination, housing discrimination, and educational discrimination among the most prominent and pressing. And they are not wrong. History shows it. Statistics bear it out. There is an issue.

The other side of the issue, though, is the one that members of the majority culture (white people) argue—the issue of personal responsibility. Each person is responsible for his or her own actions and the resulting consequences or rewards. Obey the law, this side often argues, and no harm will come to you. Work hard and you will earn. If you don't like the public schools in your area, work hard, earn, then move to a better area. Don't blame the system for your shortcomings or struggles. Take responsibility. Again, they're not wrong. Each of us is responsible for our decisions. Each of us should work hard, obey the law, and pursue opportunities.

Here we arrive at the point of conflict, the irresistible force meeting the immovable object. My simplistic description is still enough to show why this issue cannot be resolved with binary thinking, by arguing one side versus the other. Hundreds of years of cultural failure and malfunction have created a situation that cannot be resolved by shifting blame to the system or telling people to buck up and do better. Those in the minority culture cannot succeed by playing the victim and those in the majority culture are ignorant if we think there isn't a systemic problem that we are at least tangentially connected to and in part responsible for.

Whose fault is this mess? Who is responsible to fix it? All of us.

How? I don't know and neither does anyone else. Different people know different pieces of the solution—political, social, neighborly, community driven, relational, religious. Only by being actively curious can we begin to work through this.

A curious Christian, though, will not give up. We cannot shrug off complex issues, no matter how emotionally or socially charged they are. We cannot. We must identify these systemic sins, no matter our culture, and seek a right response. It is not easy. It will bring resistance both from inside and outside the church. And we must be okay with that because curiosity seeks truth and its sister, justice.

Culture is deep and wide, both our own and everyone else's. It is a wealth of discovery for the curious with numerous expressions and outlets. Each one is a collective result of fallen image bearers living together and forming societies. Each has a set of values and ways of creative expression. Each has its own stories and its own skeletons in the closet. And each is made of real individuals, and those are our connection points. We can learn much of culture at the macro level by studying, but when we form relationships across cultural lines we do more than learn *about* their culture. We learn to value it because "it" is made up of persons we value. And we begin to see our own culture in the light of another.

Media

Media is a massive category of stuff. It encapsulates social media, a significant portion of our lives, and mass media such as television, radio, print, and the web versions of each. Curiosity about media should be those questions that lead us to greater discernment. Media content is so pervasive, so all-encompassing that we easily become desensitized to its power and poison. I don't mean that all of it is poisonous. I mean that there is simply so much of it that without active, discerning curiosity we cannot determine what is poison and what is true. We lose God's truth in the detritus and we fail to protect against the lies.

If curiosity is driven by questions, what kinds of questions should we be asking about media? Maybe a better place to start is to consider whether we ever ask any questions at all. Many of us have become passive recipients of media, cisterns collecting whatever flows our way. We just sit and let it wash over and into us. Such a position is the easiest to take but also the most mindless and the least God-honoring. Curiosity is active. It seeks truth. So what kinds of questions should we ask?

How Does This Shape My Life?

Do we even consider how media shapes us? This requires a fair bit of self-awareness, the ability to step outside our present experience and examine the impact of our consumption and interaction. We need to look at the time we spend on social media or consuming other forms of media (Netflix, Hulu, Amazon Prime, news, YouTube, podcasts, etc.). We need to audit what we are exposed to—violence, sex, negativity, criticism, cynicism, beauty, art, meaningful stories, hope, thought provocation. Each of these is an ingredient of our state of mind and feeds our heart in some way, either as nutrition or poison. Our lives are more shaped by media than we realize, and we should bring curiosity to bear on it.

What Is This Taking from Me?

As we consider how media shapes us, we will realize that every engagement with it withdraws something from us. It withdraws minutes or hours. It withdraws mental energy. It withdraws emotions and feelings. It withdraws attention. It withdraws opportunities to do something else with our time and energy. Just like with money, sometimes withdrawals are necessary and good. Sometimes, though, we withdraw too much too often and find ourselves in the red. Like a bank these withdrawals can lead to overdraft fees too—just more subtle ones. We find ourselves tired, stressed, without time, and pulled away from more important pursuits.

What Is It Giving Me?

Just as media makes withdrawals from us, it leaves a deposit in their place. It deposits outlooks, feelings, facts, opinions, encouragement, insult, negativity, hope—something. Often we are so caught up in the medium that we miss the message; we don't realize the effect it is having on us. We neither appreciate its benefits nor do we recognize its dangers. So we must ask what we are gaining from our media consumption. The answer does much to determine its value for us.

I don't mean this to sound like a "beware the evils of the idiot box" soapbox sermon. Media, in all its forms offers incredible benefits. It is a remarkable information source for everything from current events to history to, well, just about anything. It inspires; think of the way certain films or documentaries or news stories make you feel, stories of activists or bravery or generosity. Media can wow us and make us happy; it can be pure entertainment. Media can absolutely be a net positive in our life. All I am asking is that we be careful *what* it is adding to our lives.

How Do I Know This Is Trustworthy?

Every media outlet has a slant. Every person has presuppositions. This means that every bit of media you consume is coming from a perspective and aiming at something. Do you know what it is? Do you know that you can trust it? FOX News calls itself "fair and balanced" and they are exactly right for everyone who falls into their target demographic. MSNBC is equally fair and balanced to the opposing target demographic. News media exists in a world with competing goals: report the news and drive ratings. The latter often influences or even overrules the former. This means not all "news" is trustworthy. Are you curious enough to dig a little deeper, find another side to the story, and learn all you can about a news story? Are you aware of the slant so you can know the inherent holes in reporting and storytelling?

Almost nothing shared on social media as news should be trusted. I get most of my news through social media, but I accept almost none of it at first blush, and neither should you. Look for other outlets reporting the same thing. Spend ninety seconds on Google. Verify the facts as well as you can. Try to learn the rest of the story, and I assure you there almost always is a rest of the story. Simply apply a little discerning curiosity to see what is true and what is not and always keep in mind that "true" means factual but also "in line with what God intends reality to be."

What Worldview Is This Espousing?

You don't need to be able to define or articulate worldviews to answer this question. You simply need to have a level against which to gauge them. You need to know what is and isn't biblical, what is and isn't honoring to Jesus. You need to have a radar that will go off when something is not quite right. And when the level is off or the radar pings, you need to ask why. What is out of whack? What doesn't add up? If you seek out answers to those questions, you will gain both a better understanding of worldviews and truth. Trust that twinge of an uncomfortable feeling telling you something is not quite right then go looking for what it might be. If you actively do this, your radar will become more sensitive and accurate, but if you suppress those feelings, that twinge, you will end up with no radar whatsoever.

Do I See God's World Better Because of This?

Does what I have consumed help me love God more by showing me truths or perspectives I had not otherwise seen? Does it reveal something of humanity to me to help me be compassionate or caring? Does it move me in some way? Did it connect me with other people or show me truth? Did it lift my spirits and point me on a good trajectory? Did it correct an assumption or wrong belief I held? While not everything we consume will answer each of these questions positively, they should be our aim.

Some will read this and think I am saying we should only read Christian fiction and watch Christian films. Good gravy, no. All that will do is turn you into a sheltered, unrealistic, fearful idealist with no concept of the real world or how to function in it. If you are a discerning person you can learn much of God, of people, of God's creation through distinctly non-Christian stories and depictions of reality too.

Pat Conroy died in early 2016. He was the author of *The Great Santini, The Water Is Wide, The Lords of Discipline, Prince of Tides,* and several other novels. His books are a glimpse into the true state of the striving human mind and heart, the pursuit of happiness and quest for fulfillment. He shows how pain breaks people down and becomes a life-long haunting enemy. And he shows glimpses of the happiness and joy that can be found, ever so fleetingly, in a hurting life. Conroy's books are not for the thin-skinned or faint of heart. They don't promote a worldview a Christian should love or embrace. But that's precisely why they need reading. They are true to life, true to experience, true to the emptiness all around us.

If you've seen *The Dark Knight,* then Heath Ledger's performance as the Joker is certainly imprinted on your mind. It was a depiction of a villain whose only aim is chaos. It wasn't a classic story of good versus evil in which the bad guy is trying to rob a bank or murder someone and the good guy is playing the hero. It's the story of a villain who simply loves wreckage, a paradigm that bends our minds and expands our thinking about the nature of evil and the good that tries to overcome it.

Both of these examples along with myriad others are depictions of evil or pain that can and do positively shape our understanding of God's world and our place in it. All we need is a little curiosity to find the good among the bad.

On Being "Cultured"

There's a term for people well versed in art and literature: *cultured.* When I hear this term I tend to think of coffee-sipping, ascot-wearing snobs or of V-neck-T-shirt-sporting, fedora-wearing, scarf-adorned hipsters in thick-framed glasses. But that's not entirely fair. Literature and art build cultures. They are the expressions of a developed culture, for better and worse. They express the values a culture holds. So to be cultured, in its truest sense, is to be tapped into the current of culture. It's more than being versed in who painted what and which books released recently. It's not being the first to know about new musicians or to have attended a foreign film festival or three. Nor is it to be encyclopedic in your knowledge of "the classics" either.

Cultured people are those who can interpret art, be it written, visual, or auditory, and explain what it expresses. They can read a culture by its art and recognize that which is of value and that which is slop or harmful. They can put their finger on how art has shaped culture and how culture has influenced art and trace both through the years. To do this one has to know what is out there and have a discerning eye and ear, but one does not have to be on the cutting edge of everything. That is an ego- or thrill-driven pursuit.

Being cultured has nothing to do with race or cultural background. It has little to do with socioeconomic status (other than the fact that wealthier people have better access to education and the opportunities and experiences it affords). Rich and poor alike can and should hunger for knowledge and truth. You can find cultured people in the halls of universities or the front stoop of a bungalow in Watts. It has everything to do with curiosity. Who is asking the right questions and seeking out the truth in the expressions of culture? These are the cultured ones, the curious people. In this sense, all of us should aspire to be cultured.

Literature and the Arts

Many of the same questions and considerations we put to media apply to literature and the arts. In our current day, media and the arts overlap significantly as delivery methods for entertainment, news, and visual or audio mediums merge into a single stream. This isn't bad. In fact it allows us to interact with material we might otherwise have completely overlooked. It does complicate matters, though, because we can no longer segment our life neatly.

For a curious person this is exciting. The merging mediums and outlets create entire new experiences and opportunities for creativity. They also raise more questions and ask even more of us. A curious person will plunge headlong into these merged streams with eagerness and heightened discernment. We will seek to discover new ways to experience truth and wonder that we never thought of before. We should ask questions like the following to see what horizons might open before us.

What Mediums Should I Gravitate toward and What Am I Missing?

I am a book person. Always have been. I will always choose the written word over video or audio. I would rather read than tour an art museum. However, if I settle for that set of choices, that dichotomy, I am diminishing my experience of God through people's creativity.

In recent years I have begun to gain an appreciation for photography (not taking photographs, mind you, just appreciating the artfulness of others). I have made friends with some songwriters, being in Nashville and all, and am fascinated by their craft. I have sought to understand book cover design and graphic design (something more authors would benefit from doing, please, I beg you). I love listening to music as a consumer and have started to pay attention to the craft of music making. I still don't love touring art museums, but I am learning to appreciate mastery and creativity in visual art forms.

I am no expert in any of these art forms and wouldn't even qualify as a novice in them. I don't bring them up to discuss my mastery—there is none—but rather point out the value of exploring and expanding our horizons. As I have explored these different mediums and expressions, I have found my capacity for enjoyment and appreciation growing. It's incredibly difficult to truly appreciate things with which we have no familiarity, so as we grow our interests find new ways to enjoy and new objects for enjoyment.

If we do not expand our horizons, we are missing out on God's expressions of beauty. The written word is not better than a sculpture or a chord progression. We should not judge a book by its cover, but an artful cover is *art*—and good marketing. If we do not expand our horizons, we are missing out on the people who love those horizons and the artists who create them.

Literature and art connect people. When I ask my songwriter friends questions about their inspiration, their craft, and their process, I am tapping into something they love. I am honoring their expertise and passion. I am connecting and relating. I am learning about their work and their humanity. That is meaningful. And the same goes when they ask about me, my writing, or my podcasting. It isn't a conversation about "So, what do you do for work?" like the awkward small talk shared at block parties or school functions we attend for our kids. We are sharing bits of ourselves.

Just as we see bits of other people and connect with them in new mediums, so too we can see bits of God. God wired each of us in a way that gravitates toward certain expressions of truth and beauty, and that multiplicity is on purpose. My proclivity for the written word should enhance and be enhanced by your proclivity for film or music or graphic design or photography. We should learn from each other and in so doing learn something of how God reveals Himself. We should see God's hand at work both in the artists' process of creativity and in their finished work.

We cannot let our preferences limit our experiences. God made us varied, and curiosity should drive us to experience and appreciate the variations. We will be richer for it in friendship, knowledge, and faith.

On Books

> The more that you read, the more things
> you will know. The more that you learn, the
> more places you'll go.[31] —Dr. Seuss

Nothing has grown and shaped my curiosity like books. I do not think there is a single medium in the world that so effectively shares information, opens new worlds, and ignites the imagination as books. It would seem you agree since you are, after all, reading or listening to a book. Books are largely what made me want to write. Books have shaped my perspectives on God, friends, sports, civil issues, faith, church, art, and nearly everything else. I read for fun and I read to learn. My greatest risk in reading is that I will collect knowledge but do not act on it, that I will become a card catalog of knowledge instead of being intent on bringing my curiosity to bear in the world.

I have friends who say things like "I really only read nonfiction." For some it's a matter of not connecting emotionally with a fictional world. For others it's a matter of investing in facts, in what is "true." They see fiction as a fanciful, fruitless, fatuous waste of time.

Here's the thing: fiction can be truer than facts. A good novel reveals the real in a way an essay or a biography usually fails to do. A novel *shows* truth; it presents a deeper layer of truth that, if described, would be boring at best and unrecognizable at worst. But when we find it woven in a story, we know it to be true. Good versus evil, nobility, honesty, courage, friendship, self-sacrifice—these are truths that fiction reveals in a way nonfiction often struggles to do.

Have you ever read a sentence then sat back and breathed out real slowly because, wow, it was just that incredible? It packed so much beauty, so much truth into just a few words. For lovers of great writing, these are transcendent, pinnacle moments like the way musicians will play back a bridge or chorus over and over again or film buffs will rewatch a scene twenty times out of sheer amazement at the camera work or cinematography. Not all readers are lovers of great writing, though. Many are lovers of information whether or not artfulness and craftsmanship are present. And yet others are reluctant readers. They know they ought to read and enough people recommended a book that they decided to soldier through it.

If you are in the first group, I hope this book meets your expectations. If you are in one of the latter two groups, I challenge you with this: explore what makes great writing great; seek out the best. Find a few favorites—authors who wow you, stories that draw you in or move your soul, genres you gravitate toward. Reading is about more than just message; it is about method too. It is about the means by which a message is communicated. There is truth communicated in both substance and style, and often substance without style actually diminishes the message. The craft of writing displays God's fingerprints.

> Books are the quietest and most constant of friends; they are the most accessible and wisest of counselors, and the most patient of teachers.[32] —Charles William Eliot

For the curious, or for the aspiring curious, books are a treasure trove. You can start almost anywhere. Pick a subject, pick a style, pick a length, pick an era in history, then grab a book and read. Read a little bit at a time. Find what you like and go.

For those who are already readers, find something new. If you love nonfiction, read fiction. If you love novels, read a biography. If you love both, read poetry.

In reading you'll learn what you set out to learn and along the way you will absorb truth and beauty in unexpected ways. Your brain will latch on to things you never suspected and remind you of them at unexpected times. If you find a book you love and find another person who loves it too, you have found a friend. Books are a curious person's greatest treasure and the gateway to experiences, people, and knowledge. So dig in.

On Music

At their bases books communicate messages. At its base music communicates raw emotion. Its sound waves and arrangements are designed to move us at a visceral, hard-to-explain level, and that is powerful. Consider movie soundtracks. They are precisely mastered and edited to move your emotions, to cue you as to how to feel in a given scene. A movie with no music often feels flat or incomplete (though the lack of soundtrack, the silence, can be used to great effect). The music swells and crescendos or dwindles to just a whisper as a guide for your emotions.

We were successful because we were curious guys.[33] —Paul McCartney

In itself music is neither moral nor immoral. It is simply organized sound, waves of noise composed and executed just so. In God's great creativity, He gave us the capacity to connect with some styles of music, some arrangements, as sad or happy or pleasant or grating. Music, this disembodied thing, merges with the human ear and mind to communicate truths even though, unlike the written word, no verbalized message of truth is attached to music. While different genres of music express different emotions and elicit different feelings, no one is more moral than the others. Neither is music just a vehicle that lyrics take for a ride. It is a medium that truth can speak through as it reflects God's creativity through composition, performance, and our ability to appreci-ate it. Music is art in itself, beautiful, terrible, or otherwise.

Most of us enjoy music in some capacity. We enjoy how it makes us feel or reflects the feelings we already have. We put on "good mood" music or music to soothe our feelings. We have tunes we wallow in when life is hard and those we play to lift us from the doldrums. We have relaxing music and pump-up music. We listen while we work out, drive, write, cook dinner, and nearly everything else. Our lives have a soundtrack.

If music is so present in our lives, shouldn't we explore it? Shouldn't we understand it? What makes good music and what doesn't? Why do some people like bro-country while the rest of us (enlightened) folks think it is a pox? Why do one-hit wonders hit? Shouldn't we explore why we like what we like and find out what else out there we might like too? If music adds to life, wouldn't it be good to understand this elixir?

And we should know lyrics. I don't mean memorize them. I mean understand them and know what they are about. Are they true? Are they uplifting? Are they artful? Some of you will say you listen to the tune and ignore the lyrics. I believe you, but do you know what cumulative effect those lyrics have on your mind and heart over time even though you are not actively tuning in to them? Your brain is passively collecting them the way ceiling fans collect dust. Over time quite a little collection builds up.

Have you ever inventoried your emotions in regards to the music you listen to? Do you know what lifts you and what brings you down? If you do then music becomes medicine or a drug. You also find out which music has side effects—depression, anger, anxiety, ambivalence. Something as beautiful and powerful as music deserves our curiosity, our questions, our exploration.

Nature and Science

Culture, media, and art are all manmade and reflect aspects of God's hand at work. They are the handiwork of God's best creations: us. Nature, though, *is* God's creativity. It is what God made when creating the earth ex nihilo—the matter, the systems, the energy, the laws, all of it.

For a long time I viewed "science" as a subject I was thrilled to have left behind in school. It was formulas and memorization and boredom. But two things began to happen simultaneously. First I began to learn, over time and quite by accident, to revel in creation. This is a beautiful, majestic world with a million faces of beauty. I began to notice that unique feeling one gets when encountering natural beauty but without the words to quite express it. It's luxuriating, soaking, trying to eke every bit of enjoyment and beauty out of what is around you.

It happened in the Boundary Waters and the Smoky Mountains and the Armenian countryside and the waves of corn in the Midwest (yes, flyover country is beautiful too). It happened on clear, bright fall days in Illinois and bone-rattling summer thunderstorms in Tennessee. I felt it at Torrey Pines State Park in California and watching a sunrise on Pensacola Beach. I reveled because I couldn't help it.

The second thing that happened was that I began to grow in my awareness of God's handiwork. After one revels it is not a big step to realize that God made the mountains and the sun and the sea, and it was good. And from there it is just one more step to wonder and ask and explore and be amazed. Just as I saw God at work in words and music and society and art, I saw as much or more so in nature. How could I not be curious about the created world?

Every day in this world is an opportunity for amazement at what God has made. I leave for work early most days, which means I am awake for the sunrise, and every single one is different. Because God is still creative. I watch the leaves change colors each fall, and I notice that the colors differ in Tennessee from what they were where I used to live in Minnesota then Illinois, more browns and oranges and rust reds instead of burgundies and golds. Because God is still creative. When my children get ill, it is miserable, an experience every parent hates. I can do little to help them. Their little bodies spike a fever or expel their dinner. This too is God's hand at work, His creative power in the systems of the human body. They are fighting to heal themselves. Their bodies are fighting the infection or virus because God made an immune system that can detect and repel illness.

If you want your eyes opened to nature and to consider aspects of creation you never think about, there is one simple way to make it happen: Go for a walk with elementary-aged school children.

"Are there poisonous snakes in Tennessee?" Yes there are, copperheads and cottonmouths and even some rattlesnakes.

"Why does the wind blow?" Because some weather systems are high pressure and some are low pressure and the air moves from one to the other.

"Why are there so many deer in this state park?" Because the rednecks aren't allowed to shoot them here.

"Why does that log have lines inside it?" Because trees add layers as they grow and age; you can tell the age by the number of rings.

Or just watch a movie with them. I took my kids to see *The Jungle Book* not long ago, and my daughter wanted to know why the snake was wrapped around Mowgli. Now she knows how constrictors work. Have you ever thought about how constrictors work, how they slowly flex their muscled bodies around their prey so that with every exhale it can inhale just a little less? It's incredible! Kind of gross, but incredible.

> We should, to begin with, think that God leads a very interesting life, and that He is full of joy. Undoubtedly He is the most joyous being in the universe. The abundance of His love and generosity is inseparable from His infinite joy. All of the good and beautiful things from which we occasionally drink tiny droplets of soul-exhilarating joy, God continuously experiences in all their breadth and depth and richness.[34] —Dallas Willard

Just look around and let science class commence. Creation shouts at us. And the more we explore it the more of Him we see. Often our reaction is "Wow!" and that's a good start. But the curious person will then say "Why?" and "What else?" because we have yet to explore all the depths of God's creation. Quite literally, in some cases.

Scientists are still discovering fish and other organisms at the ocean depths that, to date, have existed simply because God wanted them to. So much of nature seems to exist for this reason—because God simply took pleasure in making it and watching it be. Now we get to discover these things, and as we ask and explore we will see things that exist simply for beauty, others that exist as part of a delicate ecosystem, some that are majestic, some that are disgusting but cool. In all we see the genius of the Creator. God is unbelievably smart. He's not just powerful. He is smart. Have you ever considered God's intellect? He thought of all these beings and organisms and systems and environments. And then He made them.

And it is a playground for the curious.

The Workplace

Let's make a shift from exploring the mountain tops and running through flowery meadows to your home office or a corporate boardroom. How does curiosity play a role in the workplace? In productivity? In business and commerce and trade?

The best workers are learners, those discovering new and better ways of doing things. The best leaders, the only leaders who last long, are learners. Specialists can thrive for a bit, but change outpaces specialty, so we must be learners and adapters. We must be able to think on our feet and thrive in a variety of environments. The only businesses that survive in our rapidly changing world are those that can adapt. And these things can only happen if people are curious. They ask questions like how can we do this better? What challenges will we face? Who might be able to help us with this? How can our work support other people's work? What's next? Why? Why not?

> A lot of leaders stop in their growth because
> they lose their curiosity.[35] —John Maxwell

The temptation, when things are going well in the workplace, is to keep repeating what worked before. The problem is that, while this will provide good results for a while, it never looks ahead at what's coming next. Curiosity does. It wonders how things might change and how can we prepare for it. This isn't change for change's sake but rather necessary adaptation based on discovery.

Every successful entrepreneur has been curious. What if we try this? Why isn't there one of these kinds of widgets? What if we created one? What are people's needs or desires that we can meet? Question after question leading to results.

Think of Steve Jobs, probably the most celebrated and respected creative entrepreneur of our day. What drove him to create such brilliant products, items unlike anything to have hit the market previously? Curiosity.

How did Apple come up with the interactive graphic user interface that replaced the need to type commands into DOS or some other program and completely reinvented personal computing? Curiosity.

How did the design of Apple's products stand out with such elegant simplicity from every other design? You guessed it, curiosity.

How did the iPod become *the* device for "carrying a thousand songs in your pocket"? Curiosity about customers and marketing—the same thing that turned the iPhone into the standard for smart phones.

And not just a spark of curiosity, a *discipline* and culture of it. A spark of curiosity gets you one good idea or product. But only rigorously fostered and defended curiosity turns one good product into a series of subsidiary excellent products.

Consider Pixar and the work they have done over the decades with animation and storytelling. Even their bad movies are good. The only reason we think they are bad is because they aren't as good as Pixar's best films. They have set the bar so high that we expect genius. Why? Because they have a culture of curiosity that takes storytelling and graphics and technology to places nobody else ever considered going.

Curiosity makes us better coworkers too. It connects to the work of others as we understand what they do better and how our work supports it or it supports us. Curiosity leads to personal relationships and friendships that turn a work environment into a team environment. People work better when they are happier and they are happier when they connect with and identify with coworkers and bosses. We ask questions and understand others and find new ways to work with them. Curiosity helps us overcome conflict or differing work styles because it doesn't stubbornly stick to its guns.

Emotional intelligence, EQ, is the measurement most smart organizations use to measure a person's ability to effectively understand and interact with coworkers. Simply put, people who have it are curious whether they realize it or not. They are curious about how to understand others, what others are thinking, how to communicate more effectively, and what type conflict resolution will connect best. EQ measures a person's interpersonal curiosity, and people who rate poorly are simply not curious. They don't think about others. They can't picture how another person thinks, feels, or will react in a certain situation. They don't care to understand how to handle conflicts better or can't even see that they need to. EQ isn't just a personality trait. It, like curiosity in general, is a practice and discipline that helps make better employees, leaders, and teammates.

Curious people create more, find better solutions to problems, overcome challenges, meet needs that arise, make connections, and prepare better for the future. These traits are in no way tied to work style or traits like introversion or extroversion. They are not dependent on a particular work style or position in an organization either. A curious custodian can make a noticeable difference in the work environment. A curious accountant can save a company thousands or millions of dollars. A curious sales person can build fantastic relationships with accounts. A curious editor can make a publication shine. A curious CEO can connect with employees at every level and take a company to places nobody ever considered.

Curiosity can be boisterous and verbal, or it can be quiet and determined. It can work out questions in the quiet of solitude or in an open work area with a team of people. (Though, to be frank, not much can *really* be accomplished in an open office setup.) Regardless, the results will be the same: a happier and more productive work environment producing and creating at a higher level.

The Boundaries

One thing determines whether something is out of bounds for a Christian's curiosity: does it honor God? Just that.

When my parents used to ask me why I wanted to see a movie or read a book or do something with friends, this is what they were asking—does it honor God? What I saw them model was that all types of topics and interests could be engaged in a God-honoring way.

Every one of the topics I touched on in this chapter has its own books written to explore its depths. My aim was not to offer exhaustive research into culture or media or art or science or work but rather to help you see *how* curiosity fits in each. Other authors have expressed the results of their own curiosity with brilliance and at length about every single area of life I have touched on.

All you need to do is find the one that scratches where you itch and dig in. None of them is out of bounds. None of them is lesser. Yes, each one has aspects that are unsavory and must be handled with care, and yes, our curiosity can be driven by wrong motives or become drawn to mere stimulation instead of truth. But godly curiosity sees the unsavory and learns precisely what must be done with it. It does not shy away so others can stumble into it; it points it out or works to remove it.

Our curiosity is for a purpose—to honor the Lord our God with all our hearts and souls and minds and to love our neighbors as ourselves. How can we rightly do these things unless we learn about God's creation and the people He made in His image? Curiosity leads us deeper into the two greatest commandments. We need not be bound by artificial and incorrect boundaries of sacred and secular or trite and meaningful.

Go and be curious about all things so that you better love those engaged in them. Go and dig deep so that you can see God at work more clearly. Your heart, soul, and mind will be filled when you do. And not only will they be filled, their capacity will grow so that your love for God and others expands too—now and for all of life.

Chapter 6
Taking Curiosity Somewhere

People say: idle curiosity. The one thing that curiosity cannot be is idle.[36] —Leo Rosten

WE LEFT OFF LAST chapter with "just ask"—just find what interests you and ask good questions. To be transparent, that was an attempt to keep you from fleeing this book after the lengthy flyover we did of culture, media, art, nature, and work. My hope was that your eyes would be lifted to new distances and expanses and your curiosity might be fueled toward something you hadn't considered previously or might have felt guilty about.

Really, though, "just ask" isn't a terribly helpful piece of advice. If you were planning a road trip and asked a friend, "So, what do I do first?" you wouldn't want them to say, "Drive." But that's kind of what I just did, and now I want to make it up to you by helping you figure out where the real starting point for curiosity is and what to do with it.

Who Are You?

> You must have an enormous appetite for
> humanity and for life and for the world.
> You really have to feel like you cannot
> fill yourself up enough with this amazing
> place we live in. If you have that feeling,
> like sincerely have it, you'll do okay.[37]
> —Sebastian Junger

If you can't answer this question, it's a good starting place for applying curiosity. Do you know your strengths and weaknesses? Do you know what you love and what you hate? Do you know where you draw energy and what enervates you?

Are you curious about yourself?

These are important questions for understanding how God designed you uniquely and what trajectory might be best for you.

Such questions can't be answered in isolation very easily. We judge ourselves both too harshly and too graciously. We have more blind spots about our own lives than anything else, so we need help. We need help from peers and mentors, so ask them what they see in you.

What stands out? What is strong? What is weak? We need help from experts, so take two or three evaluations like Strengths Finder[38] and Myers-Briggs.[39] Take a spiritual gifts test such as the one in *Discover Your Spiritual Gifts*[40] by C. Peter Wagner. None of these will define you, but they will help you understand you. Each provides a piece of the puzzle as to why you are the way you are, where you will thrive, and what you should do next.

While you're exploring the basics of who you are, take inventory of two things, what you enjoy and who you know. Make a list of the things you would do if you had a year of unhindered free time and resources to match, what books you would read, places you'd visit, movies you'd watch, activities you'd participate in, foods you love and foods you'd like to try. Write down the things from your past that leave the fondest memories and that you'd like to do again. Then start writing down the names of friends and family. Write down interesting people you've met. Write down people you notice, or types of people, even if they're strangers or have caught your attention through their work.

I have lived and worked in or around cities most of my life. I grew up in inner-city Minneapolis then lived in the suburbs of Chicago and now live on the outskirts of Nashville. I have worked in the heart of both Chicago and Nashville. Cities thrill me—the energy, the people, the hum. For me, cities have provided my starting point because they provide such a variety of vibrant cultures and experiences. It is a pleasure to sit on a park bench or in a coffee shop and watch hundreds of people stream by. It sparks questions and engages the imagination to explore cities.

But the same is true of a small town. A town-square diner where the old men gather to shoot the breeze and gossip like old ladies is no less fascinating than Midtown Manhattan. They're just different flavors. A North Dakota farming community is no less energizing than Sunset Boulevard. They just offer different opportunities. Which one is yours? Which are you close to? Which sparks something in you?

Every interest of yours is a potential connection point for you and each tells you something about yourself. You enjoy those things for a reason. Those people are in your life or your mind for a reason. As you take these inventories, different things will rise to the top. Take note! They may be your starting place.

Finally consider how you work and learn. Take what you know of yourself and/or what those evaluations revealed and think about how you do your best work. How do you absorb information? How do you process it? Is it through hearing, seeing, reading, or hands-on experience? Do you work best with others or in isolation? Do you enjoy bouncing from thing to thing or honing in on one project or subject and seeing it through?

Some of you will have little difficulty with these questions and tasks. You already know your Myers-Briggs personality type and could describe the perfect work environment. Others will feel like I just assigned a capstone project for graduating from college. It's all *so much*. This says something about your respective personalities, and that's something to note too. I'm not trying to give an assignment but rather to give a few steps to take to help you understand yourself well enough to know what direction your curiosity should be pointed. You do not need to find *the* entry to curiosity because there isn't just one. There are millions, so you just need to find the one closest to you.

Choose Your Curiosity Wisely

All these questions and inventories aren't some sort of algorithm. They will not offer a curiosity horoscope telling you what you can expect. They simply help you understand what you're good at and what you enjoy, and that is enough to shape your sense of curiosity. In fact, by inventorying what you love and who you know, you have a treasure trove of material at hand already. You do not need to be an expert in everything, and even if you wanted to be, you couldn't. Nobody can, but some of you can absolutely be experts in something.

I love the show *Justified* (mild spoiler alert). It centers on a brash, gun-slinging U.S. Marshal assigned to the state of his youth, Kentucky. Along with a number of fantastic characters and plot lines, one of the sneaky antagonists of the story is the setting—specifically the coal mines of eastern Kentucky. They are hideouts for outlaws, stashes for stolen goods, booby traps for unsuspecting suckers, and access points to bank vaults. Throughout the show, the mines are spoken of with fear and respect because of the shafts that run hundreds of feet into the ground. They are narrow, just three or four feet wide, and have no visible bottom.

An expert is a lot like that, minus the threat of death and the proximity to outlaws. Expertise is a deep, narrow look into one subject. It drills way down into the depths and mines all it can. It doesn't diverge from its subject and it rarely intersects with another area of interest or learning. Make no mistake, this is a kind of curiosity because it is constantly asking "What else?" and "What's next?" And we need experts. We need those who know all that's humanly possible about different topics.

This kind of curiosity is just right for some people; it's their entry point and their path. As they answer the "Who am I?" and "How do I work best?" questions, they gravitate to research and the deep dive. Most of us, I think, are not so focused. Most of us will find our curiosity aroused by the things that cross our paths on a daily basis. We simply need to be attentive, to *notice*. Noticing is hard work.

It means listening well for what is interesting or what strikes a funny note or informs us of something new. It means watching for the beauty, the funny, the odd, the new, the surprising, or the interesting. It means wondering as we watch and listen. What's her story? She seems sad. Where did that come from? I've never noticed it before and it seems out of place. Where is that accent from? I can't quite place it. I wonder why he got that tattoo on his leg? Charlie Brown seems an odd name choice for a grown man. What did that building used to be? It's a bar now but it looks like it might have been a bank once upon a time. Noticing is a muscle and the more we do it the stronger it gets. Flex it, notice, and then latch on to whatever grabs your attention and be curious about it.

All of us, expert and noticer alike, must be thinkers. Curiosity has a reputation as a childish trait because we stopped using our minds. We stopped looking at life, the mundane and normal, as something worth our brain waves. We ignore it and it rolls over us like surf over a beached, bloated whale. When we fail to notice and engage, that's about how lively and spry our minds are. We walk through it as if it's not there. But we don't think about it. But thinking *is* curiosity. It's what we looked at last chapter in all those areas of life. Nothing is out of bounds so long as our curiosity honors God and loves others.

For all of us this thinking, this intentional curiosity, is what connects us to ideas and those ideas to real people. It's what connects person to person as we ask questions and hear each other's stories and learn from one another. Curiosity is that which finds God's truth in all created things and beings and figures out how it fits in life and the greater world. It rejects the premise of "mindless entertainment" and actively rebels against passively walking through life. Whether we are inclined to be the expert or the noticer, we take to life actively, full of questions, seeking to find and show truth and beauty.

Broad or Focused

I think curiosity is everything. It's the underlying motivation to learn. It's a characteristic where you acknowledge you don't know everything and perhaps there are better ways to do things. I'm always nervous about people who aren't curious about anything in the world.[41] —Simon Sinek

We need both experts and noticers; neither is at their best without the other. Experts, as we described earlier, are mine shafts into specific disciplines or areas of knowledge. They are deep divers who unearth all that can be found about a topic be it theology, baseball statistics, or macroeconomics. A true expert doesn't collect knowledge then stop; she continues to look at her subject from different angles and ask different questions to see what else might be learned.

The noticer, on the other hand, is a bit of a dabbler. He finds bits and pieces of information about many things. He notices interesting and worthwhile truths all over the place and takes note of them, but rarely does he dig in deep. Some noticers have expert leanings and will settle down on an interesting topic to take a close look, or maybe they continue to come back to the same thing time and again because it is so important or compelling. And of course most experts are not single-minded automatons attached to one discipline. This is not an either/or (Binary Thinking Alert) but a continuum, a scale based on preference and proclivity just like introversion and extroversion and other personality traits. But the further along the spectrum you go in one direction or the other, the more you find the desire to dig deep or to find the new.

Michael Lewis, a journalist and author, exemplifies this very spectrum well in his fantastic book *Moneyball*. It is the story of how the Oakland Athletics front office had to find ways to compete in Major League Baseball while handcuffed by a small budget and lack of resources compared to top teams like the Yankees or Red Sox. Lewis describes how the A's began to use statistical analysis of player production in areas of the game other teams overlooked. They found under-appreciated assets, acquired them inexpensively, and built a winning team.

What is remarkable about *Moneyball* is that it is much more a story of curiosity and a display of deep curiosity by Lewis than it is a mere baseball story. Billy Beane, the A's general manager, was curious enough to find new solutions that were innovative for their time (and have since been adopted by most MLB teams) by taking an area of research—statistical analysis—and applying it in a fresh way. He was a noticer and his assistant GM, Paul DePodesta, was an expert. Together they created a dynamic whole. Lewis was curious enough to research this story, to notice different threads of narrative, to learn baseball and statistics well enough to explain both to common readers. He both dug deep and noticed widely and the result was a delightful and informative read. And the final layer is that readers of the book who wanted a fun baseball story got that, but they also got an education in various leadership and business principles that could be applied in ways they might not have anticipated.

Both experts and noticers need the other because they are the perfect complement to one another. The weakness of the expert is that she knows an inordinate amount about one topic but isn't sure exactly what to do with it. Who needs it? What might the applications for this knowledge be? What implications might this knowledge have for other disciplines or industries? They know the stuff, but not the people and the needs and opportunities.

The noticer is just the opposite. He sees enough of the world to recognize needs and possibilities. He finds a problem but lacks a solution. He finds an opportunity but isn't sure exactly how to take advantage of it. But when a noticer meets an expert, or finds her work, magic can happen. He can help her take that expertise and put it to use. She can meet a need he found but couldn't do anything about.

A practical example of this is book recommendations. I am much more noticer than expert and I read across quite a few genres but am not an expert in any one of them. By reading a little from many genres I get a sense of who knows what. Along the way my love for books has connected me with other readers and authors, some of whom are experts. So when someone reaches out and asks, "What's the best book on _____?" I can either give them a recommendation I've read that was written by an expert or I can ask an expert I know to suggest something.

My noticing connects an expert with a need and both the asker and the answerer are better for it. I'm not capable of offering an annotated bibliography, but I can often point the way to someone who can.

Information vs. Curiosity

August 1, 1981 is a date that shaped an entire generation, whether or not we know it. On that day MTV launched with the music video "Video Killed the Radio Star" by the Buggles. MTV became one of the most powerful entertainment forces throughout the 80s and 90s. They launched and elevated careers. They helped popularize reality TV. They were a force despite the fact that they didn't really, actually kill off radio hits with their music videos.

For the current generation it seems an apt parallel might be "Google killed the curious mind." Google is the evil empire making us all dumber, ruining education, and providing easy answers to hard questions. Instead of thinking, we type, and we're all worse for it. Smart phones for dumb people, right?

Certainly we live in a day with more information available more easily than at any time in history. Cities used to be known for their libraries. Universities were known for their collections of written works. Now we carry gigabytes of memory and almost unimaginable computing power in our pockets. Several of the quotes you've read throughout this book were found through a simple Google search, citations and all. We can connect to this magical electronic web of information from just about anywhere except my grandma's house in rural Georgia. It is remarkable the information we have; it's truly the information age.

Humans always gravitate toward the easiest option. We do what's easiest, so naturally we're going to use Google instead of memorizing stuff. Does that make this generation, with knowledge in their pockets instead of their backpacks and lockers, dumber? Probably a little bit when it comes to memorizing information, but absolutely not when it comes to having answers. We have more ability now to solve problems, discover truth, and make connections than ever before. Time will tell how our minds are affected by this new way of learning (or not learning, as the case may be), but it is unfair to accuse people of being dumber because of the Internet.

This access can fool us into thinking we are smarter than we are, though. It allows us to think less and search more. We are lazy, so why think when we could ask Siri to look something up for us? A nasty by-product of this can be that we lose curiosity. Why ask and notice when all we need to know is at our fingertips?

Except that Google should be a super power for the curious person! Rather than deadening our minds, it should open up a world of opportunities. We have answers to questions readily at hand, which means we can ask new and better questions and learn even more. No longer is "I don't know" an acceptable answer in most cases. The Internet is a universe in itself with so much to observe and engage.

Having information and being curious should feed one another, grow one another. Information is the fuel of curiosity. Curiosity is active and intentional. It uses available tools to their fullest extent and finds new ways to use them. It doesn't let answers sit out there unused and undiscovered.

Curiosity sees the world of Internet interaction as one worth understanding and engaging just like other aspects of culture and society. Curiosity sees that the Internet is not just a hub of information; it is a hub of human connections, and it plunges in headlong to better grasp them and make the most of them. Remember, curiosity seeks to love our neighbor as ourselves and be shaped by the fruits of the Spirit.

The thing about curiosity is that it sees endless opportunities for discovery, for learning, for relationship. It seeks truth in all places.

Where others declare doom, it looks for light and opportunity. It does not settle for the easy or lazy. It takes action with heart and mind with whatever means, whatever methods, and whatever propensities the curious one has at his or her disposal.

Becoming

Who you are, whether you have yet discovered it or not, is no accident. God made you with certain gifts and tendencies. He made you to excel in certain areas and not as much in others. Then He put you in a context that has shaped those gifts and tendencies into who you are and put you on a trajectory toward who you are becoming.

We are not static beings. Yes, we have innate characteristics, but we are always changing either for better or worse. Curiosity rightly applied determines which. Are we pursuing the right things so that we progress or the wrong things so we regress? Are we investing in truth so that our minds and hearts grow and expand or are we wasting those same minds so that our souls atrophy?

Curiosity, whether applied broadly as a noticer or specifically as an expert, is an ability God has given us to help us become.

We start by asking "Who am I?" and as we answer that question we will also see more clearly who we would like to become. We will see both the strengths we want to bolster and the weaknesses we need to correct. We will see the good God is working in us and the sins we need His help overcoming. In this way curiosity is a catalyst for spiritual growth, not quite a spiritual discipline but something that enhances all of our spiritual disciplines.

Who are you? Who are you becoming?

Active curiosity will help you find the answers.

Chapter 7

Curiosity without Fear

Curiosity has occasionally gotten me in trouble. But even when curiosity has gotten me in trouble, it has been interesting trouble.[42] —Brian Grazer

CURIOSITY KILLED THE CAT.

If only. A few years ago my family got a puppy as a Father's Day present for me. I love dogs and was thrilled. Unfortunately we found out over the next two days that my youngest daughter, a toddler at the time, was miserably allergic to Belle the black lab. So we had to choose, Belle or the baby. We chose the baby.

I abhor cats. I believe cats are what Satan did to dogs at the fall. It's not explicit in Genesis, but if you squint, cross your eyes, read closely, do a little numerology, and hang out with a cat for three days, you'll see it. So when I got an email that a former coworker had a litter of kittens she was giving away for free, I hit delete faster than I do on the emails from Prince Ahmed of Nigeria promising me untold millions. Free is too high a price to pay for a cat.

But then I saw my daughters' faces. I saw their sadness at returning Belle and the gladness they'd have at getting a kitten (a cute word for cats that haven't yet become evil). So I undeleted the email, got details, and went and picked up a little gray fluff ball that has since brought much joy to everyone in the family but me. They're all insane, by the way. I love them all, but they are insane.

Over time I have seen where the phrase "curiosity killed the cat" came from. Not because our cat has died, but because she is incapable of resisting every nook, cranny, ledge, doorway, box, suitcase, and other opening or hidey place. She is incapable even if she already tried it four times already that same day—into the closet she goes to smell my shoes and hide in the laundry. This leads to weekly "where is the cat" games that unfortunately we keep winning. She was locked in the pantry. She was locked outside. She's under the bed hunting a spider that might be a Brown Recluse. She is behind the TV cabinet eating an electric cord. And so on.

At this rate curiosity is high on the list of things that will kill the cat ranking right behind old age and just ahead of me.

Curiosity Did NOT Kill the Christian

Many people view curiosity in this light, as something that leads people into precarious places and down risky paths. It gets us into trouble and tempts us to stick our nose where noses have no business being. They warn of the landmines and pitfalls. And they're not entirely wrong.

When we look around us at the world, especially from the place of Christian morals, it is a cesspool, a veritable Sodom and Gomorrah. The world is full of ugly and awful and offensive. It is an unjust, unclean, poisonous place in millions of ways. Being a Christian in this place can be scary and fear is why some warn against curiosity. It's a slippery slope, they say.

Only if you decide to go sledding.

At the risk of stating the obvious, we aren't cats. We don't have to go through every open door and climb to the highest point of everything. We don't have to pounce on everything that moves. We don't follow our noses. We have minds and souls, not just animal instincts. For us, curiosity is a habit, an exercise, a mental and spiritual muscle. It is the exercise of discernment. Ultimately it is an act of worship and a deep reflection of our humanity, God's nature reflected in us.

I hesitate to use the word *discernment* because angry bloggers have co-opted the term and turned it into something ranging from unpleasant to outright malicious and sinful. But they do the term a disservice. Discernment is the ability and practice of seeing and deciding what is right and what is wrong, what is good and what is bad. It is a sense and practice. And that is what mature, godly, truth-seeking curiosity leads to.

> Finally brothers, whatever is true, whatever is honorable, whatever is just, whatever is pure, whatever is lovely, whatever is commendable—if there is any moral excellence and if there is any praise—dwell on these things. (Phil. 4:8)

What is true? What is honorable? What is just? What is pure? What is lovely? In our world it can be hard to tell. Almost nothing is black and white, especially not people. Motives are not. Stories are not. Products are not. Businesses are not. Politics are not. Entertainment is not. Church is not. Cultures are not. In nearly every interaction we must be able to *discern* what is pure and lovely, what is honorable and true and conversely what is not.

Curiosity is how we do that. We wonder and ask from a place of truth seeking.

All In

The same people who consider curiosity a dangerous or foolish endeavor are the ones who want to keep their distance from the world—and start discernment blogs about all things worldly. They mistake all things in the world for all things worldly. They see it is as a sin to "dabble" in the world, to get too close. In this they miss the complexity and beauty, the threads of good and fallen woven through all of creation. They write off much of what is true, honorable, just, pure, lovely, and commendable because of its proximity to that which isn't.

> Everything in life conspires against our sense of wonder: age, experience, our jobs, even our church.[43] —Andy Stanley

Getting close enough to examine the things of earth isn't sinful any more than a doctor examining for cancer is a poor lifestyle decision by him. Staying or returning to them once we know they're sinful is. Our curiosity, if godly, is not the thing that leads us into sin. It's the thing that helps us recognize it.

Jesus calls His followers to be in the world as He was, but not of the world. We are to be *of* His Kingdom, defined by it and living according to its standards.

We are called to go into all the world and make disciples.

We are called to be all things to all people.

We are called to be shrewd as serpents and harmless as doves.

We are called to love our neighbors as ourselves.

But how in the world can we do these things if we are not in the world? How can we know our neighbors unless we move into the neighborhood? Or connect with people or learn cultures or be shrewd or be all things without being close enough and invested enough to learn what those things are? We cannot without being curious. Curiosity is a primary tool for fulfilling the mission of Christ. Without it we are distant from and clueless about those who need Jesus most.

To follow these commands, we must understand both what Christ's Kingdom demands and what the world needs. We must be fully *in* the world, bringing the kingdom to it. Curiosity and the discernment it begets enable us to plunge into culture, to soak in it, but not be defined or shaped by it. It gives us eyes to see all the potential intersection points with people through work, entertainment, interests, and the rest of life.

Without curiosity we would either be not in the world at all—cloistered hermits having no influence for the Kingdom—or we would be fully of it, consuming everything the world offers with no thought or filter. But with curiosity we can be fully in the world but fully of Christ's Kingdom.

The Evil Temptress

If you are like me, a little voice in the back of your head—likely one that sounds like a Southern revival preacher—is screaming his fool head off about the evils and temptations of the world right now. He is bellowing about Babylon and hellfire and the wiles of the devil. Or maybe you're more level-headed and haven't sat through many tent meetings and you're simply wondering about how to reconcile what I wrote earlier about the evils of the world and our call to be fully in it. It is a good question, and that fiery little preacher in my head is not entirely wrong.

The world is an evil temptress, beckoning us to our downfall. It is scintillating and intoxicating, fogging our minds and numbing our senses. Think of Vanity Fair in *The Pilgrim's Progress,* or how Emperor Palpatine tried to lure Luke Skywalker to the dark side in *Star Wars.* Remember the White Witch's Turkish delight that so entranced Edmund in *The Lion, the Witch, and the Wardrobe.* Picture the swirling, hypnotic eyes of Kaa, the snake, in *The Jungle Book.* Picture Odysseus tied to the mast of his ship, begging to be set free, while his crew packs their ears with beeswax to avoid the song of the Sirens in Homer's *Odyssey.*

So many stories tell of evil seducing people. These authors knew the appetizing, sparkling draw of temptation on people. They knew that evil draws us not by showing its true colors but by presenting itself as desirable. Even the devil is described as an angel of light. He even tried to lure Jesus into sin with promises of power and comfort.

> Again, the Devil took Him to a very high mountain and showed Him all the kingdoms of the world and their splendor. And he said to Him, "I will give You all these things if You will fall down and worship me." (Matt. 4:8–9)

No question, the evils of the world are a powerful gravitational pull for our sinful hearts. To say we are to be fully in the world denies none of this. Neither does it downplay the risks and dangers.

The Defense

> Curiosity will conquer fear even more than bravery will.[44] —James Stephens

For six chapters I have tried to explain and describe and display curiosity as a pursuit of truth, as something rooted in the character of God and digging deep into that character. When we venture into the world, we do so from a place of strength not a place of fear. We do so knowing where our strength lies, not trusting our ability to fend off temptation.

Curiosity is the very thing that anchors us in God's strength as it learns more, seeks more, and sees more of Him. And this strength is precisely the defense we need against the wiles of the world. Curiosity is the light cutting through the darkness and the breeze blowing away the fog. It is the truth that reveals the lie and the hand that pulls away the veil. It will sort out and parse the good from the bad, the beautiful from the ugly, the right from the wrong.

"The best defense is a good offense."

I don't know who said it first, but thousands of generals, admirals, and high school football coaches have co-opted it since. For those of us not in combat or on the gridiron, curiosity is such an offense; we enter the world fully on the attack. We bring the truth of God's Word to bear on the culture around us. We shine lights into dark places to discover what lies there. Will all evil flee from us? No—some will fight back, but we can be certain that we have the weapons and the power to defeat it because our curiosity is drawing on an infinitely good and powerful God, not simply our own intellects and strength of will.

Conviction versus Curiosity

Can someone be a person of conviction and a curious person at the same time? It's a pertinent question because all this talk of "in versus of" the world seems to create a tension. Stereotypically the people we think of with the most conviction are not people we would consider to be very curious. Instead of learning and seeking their motto seems to be "Here I am; I will not be moved." They're static and closed-minded, whereas curiosity is dynamic and demands movement. In short, people of conviction are boring while curious people are interesting. Clearly a conflict exists, especially when you consider that Christians *must* have conviction.

So how do we do it? How do we grow in curiosity and conviction without one cannibalizing the other?

Consider the idea of being open-minded first. Just a few sentences ago I described people of conviction as being closed-minded, and in doing so I exacerbated a false dichotomy many hold to, maybe without realizing it, that says conviction is closed-minded and open-mindedness is for fools. Few people would describe it just this way because nobody wants to think of themselves as closed-minded, but if we look at how many conservative Christians live, this is the state of things. One's convictions preclude allowing new ideas or beliefs in or even near. The alternative, then, is that to be open-minded is to have no conviction and to be swayed by whatever the latest trend or thought or discovery might be.

While juxtaposing the two sides against each other in this manner is simpler to understand, it is also untrue (as is the case most of the time when we turn something complex into an either/or—Binary Thinking Alert). True, being closed-minded means being immovable and refusing to let new ideas in. But being open-minded does not mean letting the cage of the brain open so all the birds of thought can escape. Neither does it mean being easily swayed by the winds of society.

Open-mindedness, at its best, is humility and grace blended with curiosity—but not without conviction. It means being open to listen to others, to take what they say and interpret it as graciously as possible, to consider alternative and opposing points of view to see if they have merit. It means *really* listening—listening for meaning and intent rather than just for the chance to offer a counterpoint. And it means looking for truth in what one hears.

Notice none of that requires the release of conviction. I don't need to give up on my beliefs about Jesus in order to listen graciously. Rather my beliefs about Jesus should be the very reason I listen graciously. I don't need to ignore Scripture to be curious about what other people believe. In fact, Scripture gives me security in my curiosity.

I have forgotten most of what I was taught in college, or I wasn't paying close enough attention in the first place. However a few seminal moments from lectures stick in my mind. One such moment was from a class taught by Jerry Root when he said, "I will believe anything someone can prove to me without a shadow of a doubt." My nineteen-year-old brain was bent. I had been such a stubborn, arrogant person that the thought of being persuaded to change my views was anathema to me. But what I heard from Dr. Root was both eminently reasonable and humble.

In a single sentence he explained godly open-mindedness—be willing to listen to arguments carefully and process them honestly, but do not move from a conviction without ample reason to do so.

When we are curiously open-minded in this way, we find the intersection points where the gospel connects with people. We listen for their desires, their beliefs, their passions, their pains, the holes in their lives and . . . there it is! The place the gospel connects. Through learning about people's passions and beliefs and through getting to know them by really listening, we begin to see where things we feel deepest conviction about can make a difference in their lives too.

Don Richardson, in his excellent books *Peace Child* and *Eternity in Their Hearts*, shares stories of how this so beautifully plays out. In *Peace Child*, Don tells his own family's story of going to Papua New Guinea to reach the cannibalistic Sawi people. The Sawis so highly valued treachery and deceit that when the Richardsons began to share with them the story of Jesus' life, Judas, not Jesus, was the hero. By any measure their culture was one of counter-gospel.

How could the Richardsons explain the gospel to a people whose greatest values appeared to be antithetical to gospel values? The villain was their hero. The betrayer was their archetype. Don and his wife saw a way in through a ritual the tribe held called the "peace child" in which warring tribes exchanged a child in order to make a truce. Through this ritual, the giving of a child by his father for the sake of peace, the Richardsons were able to introduce the gospel, showing how our heavenly Father gave His Son for the sake of our eternal peace. Could that have happened if they had not been open-minded, curious, looking for the cultural connection to truth?

In *Eternity in Their Hearts*, Richardson tells story after story like this one. He tells of ancient cultures the world over with rituals and prophecies and teachings that are pagan but end up being the open door for the gospel. These stories show how every culture intersects with truth somewhere. Every heart yearns for it. It takes curiosity, open-mindedness, and a lot of patience to see it often times. But it is there.

Notice the implication of this for those of us in the West. We often think we have a corner on the gospel. We think of Christian culture as Western culture and vice versa. But it is not "our" gospel. One of the greatest miracles of the gospel is that it transcends every culture. That's because it is the truth of a transcendent God who created all people. When we attach cultural values and implications to the saving truth of the gospel, we often hinder it and limit its effect for those from different cultures. The gospel is not monocultural; we are. This is why we must be curious and open-minded enough to learn other cultures and expressions of the gospel.

What we need is curious conviction. We must welcome without wavering. We must recognize that what we see is not the entirety of truth—the foundational conviction of curiosity. We must be humble enough to realize that we could be wrong, especially in our expression and application of convictions. We often are. And we must constantly be looking for where truth and people intersect because that point is where the gospel can land.

The Best Convictions

> Curiosity is, in great and generous minds, the first passion and the last.[45] —Samuel Johnson

Nobody had better, more perfect convictions than Jesus. Nobody expressed His convictions better than Jesus. He never dug in His heels when He should give nor did He ever give when firmness was needed. Jesus welcomed all without ever wavering on His mission or message. In fact, welcoming was usually His means of sharing that mission and message.

Think of Zacchaeus, the hated cheat of a tax collector. Jesus invited Himself over to Zacchaeus's home, a thing nobody did. He dined with Zacchaeus. Through that act, that connection, that simple gracious willingness to associate with him as a peer, Jesus shared the message of forgiveness and a life was changed.

Think of the woman at the well, a philandering Samaritan female—three things that would make a Jewish male of that time despise her. And yet Jesus asked her for help, talked with her, and answered her questions (even the ones designed to deflect from her sordid personal life). He was not shy about correcting her sins, but He did so in a way that led her to truth, not into a defensive or combative stance. In the end she and many in her town found salvation that day.

Think of Nicodemus, the Pharisee who had all the scriptural knowledge but not the assurance that his knowledge amounted to salvation. Jesus listened to his questions and challenged him with hard truths. Whereas He was gentle with the fragile, He was firm with the religious leader. He spoke in a manner that would be respected, as one with authority, and challenged Nicodemus. Here too the message of God's saving love for the world was shared.

In each instance, as in so many others, Jesus interacted in an open-minded way. Could He have communicated His convictions about lying and cheating to Zacchaeus and reminded him of the Ten Commandments? Could He have excoriated or shamed the woman at the well for marital failures and adultery? Could He have talked down to Nicodemus or outed him before his pompous peers for his questions? Yes, yes, and yes.

But Jesus didn't handle His convictions this way. Rather through holy open-mindedness, through good questions, through really listening, He saw where each person's life intersected with saving truth and He declared the truth at that intersection.

What we see from Jesus, throughout all of His life, is the balance of conviction and curiosity. We see how someone rooted deeply in God's Word can venture into the most lascivious of places—after all, Jesus was known for partying with the sinners of all sinners—without becoming part of the mess.

We have nothing to fear from the world if our curiosity is truly seeking God's truth and is anchored in His Word and character. We can't catch the world's evil like a cold. If our curiosity is like that of Christ, we have everything to offer the world and a way to offer it.

Chapter 8

Optimism, Skepticism, and Curiosity

EVERY MONTH OR TWO a new hoax pops up on social media, especially Facebook. Sometimes it's a bogus story about a celebrity dying. Sometimes it's one of those "repost this or Mark Zuckerberg will steal all the photos of your children and your bank account information." (Right. Because Mark Zuckerberg is hurting for money.) Sometimes it's more subtle, a quote taken out of context to misrepresent the speaker, or some statistics presented in such a way as to say the opposite of what they actually mean. My favorites are satire pieces by sites like The Onion that people take seriously and share with spiteful or fearful comments.

All this is enough to make a level-headed person fairly skeptical of "news" that shows up on social media. Many of us have learned to check the facts before sharing and to check the source before freaking out. Thirty seconds on Google saves us from propagating nonsense. This sort of skepticism is a healthy thing and extricates us from a decent amount of trouble. We'd all benefit if Aunt Beatrice could gain healthy skepticism before sharing another phony Facebook privacy notice.

We see here an instance when skepticism is a good thing. But is it in general? Is being a skeptic beneficial to faith, to relationships, to engaging culture well as a Christian? It seems, at first blush, that skepticism is a combatant with faith. If faith is the assurance of things hoped for and the conviction of things not seen, then skepticism is the questioning of those same things. Can they coexist?

Skepticism and Doubt

Doubt and skepticism are cousins, the kind of cousins who bear a family resemblance but are not as close as siblings. Both are part of the uncertainty family.

They're the kind of cousins about whom a great-aunt would comment, "My, you both look like your great-grandfather!"

Doubt is, at its base, not being certain of something. It is neither negative nor positive—it's simply a lack of knowledge. Doubt can go either way.

Skepticism is doubt with attitude. It is unsure of the facts or details but pretty sure that what it can't see isn't good. It brings its doubts to bear with bias and looks for confirmation of them.

All people doubt. That's the nature of being finite and not knowing everything. We will inevitably and daily run into situations that raise questions and cause doubt. They will occur at work, at church, in our faith, in our relationships, in our own private thoughts. Some people, though, are more inclined toward skepticism. When questions arise for these people, myself among them, they bring with them a certain negativity, almost a pessimism, telling them that the answers won't be what they want or maybe that the answers won't be discoverable at all.

What made Mr. Merrill infinitely more attractive was that he was full of doubt; he expressed our doubt in the most eloquent and sympathetic ways. In his completely lucid and convincing view, the Bible is a book with a troubling plot, but a plot that can be understood. . . . Although he knew all the best—or, at least, the least boring— stories in the Bible, Mr. Merrill was most appealing because he reassured us that doubt was the essence of faith, and not faith's opposite.[46] —John Irving, *A Prayer for Owen Meany*

Such skepticism might be a product of nature, nurture, or both. It might just be an inclination, but most often it is an inherent inclination fostered by experiences of being disappointed. Skepticism usually has self-protective roots; it expects little because having high hopes leads to disappointment as often as not.

As noted earlier, there are times when skepticism is beneficial because the world is full of things toward which we should not be trusting. But as a way of life, as a lens through which one views the world, is it beneficial?

Doubt too can be a positive thing because it raises questions, and questions are how people learn. It can lead us deeper into truth. On the other hand, doubt can devolve into skepticism over time, especially when we face repeated frustration or disappointment.

What separates the healthy from the unhealthy, the good from the bad in doubt and skepticism?

The Difference Maker

Curiosity makes the difference, of course. What else would you expect from this book?

Both doubt and skepticism are questioning mind-sets. Curiosity, or a lack thereof, determines whether these questions are healthy or not. If questions stem from a desire to find truth, to learn, to see deeper things, then either the doubt or skepticism is going to be healthy.

However, skepticism must only be exercised sparingly. It ought not be the default point of view. It is one thing to be skeptical *of* something or someone because you have reason to believe they are untrustworthy. It is something else entirely, something insidious even, to *be* a skeptic. Curiosity can be skeptical, but a skeptic will have a nearly impossible time maintaining curiosity because skepticism has a predetermined outcome it expects. It is closed-minded and has a difficult time accepting or even recognizing a different result.

This is why curiosity is so crucial. It turns our doubts into fuel for learning and discovering instead of seeds of fear or anger or bitterness. It softens our skepticism, even when it is justified, so that we can still find truth and goodness where it shows itself. And, since curiosity is the pursuit of truth, when skepticism is proven correct, curiosity gets what it came for too.

Believe All Things and Believe Nothing

Christians are to live lives marked by love—to, as 1 Corinthians 13 puts it, believe all things, hope all things, endure all things. This means we are to be defined by characteristics of grace. We are to assume the best of people and offer them the same hope and patience and mercy we know we so desperately need. We are to offer them second and third and fifty-fourth chances. In short, we are to exude the love Jesus poured out on us.

But it doesn't mean we should pull the wool over our eyes. Believing and hoping all things does not mean being gullible. It does not mean ignoring sin or injustice or wrong doing of any kind. It's not blind optimism about people. Christians must have a realistic sense of the world and its inhabitants. Yes, they are made in the image of God, but Genesis 3 did happen. People are sinners, and for all its wonders and beauty this world can be a pretty awful place. More often than not, it will disappoint us and leave us hurt.

One of my pet peeves is the use of superlatives and overstatement on the Internet in an attempt to drive traffic and increase clicks. You know, "Check out this video of the *most adorable kitten ever*" and "Whoa, this college basketball player just *went into orbit* on this dunk" and the like. Well one such phrase is particularly insidious, that about "restoring faith in humanity" as in "The way this man responds when he sees a three-legged naked mole rat will *restore your faith in humanity*." What they really mean is this will give you warm fuzzies. To be clear, warm fuzzies do not equate to faith in humanity, and if you are dumb enough to have faith in humanity you will deserve everything that comes your way. Look around. What's to have faith in? Humanity is collectively pretty awful.

We are to have faith in God and love humanity, not have faith in humanity. Humanity will be a perpetual disappointment if we do that. It will lie, cheat, steal, and desert. It is capable of remarkable good, but aside from Christ it is rooted in sin and will gravitate back to it—to selfish motives at others' expense, including you.

Yet we are to hope all things and believe all things and love our neighbors as ourselves and treat others as we want to be treated. These realities seem incongruous. How can we believe and hope all things about someone or something that we cannot and should not trust? How can we assume the best about someone while also assuming they will disappoint?

The Balance—Grace and Wonder

Somehow, some way we are to maintain optimism about people while being firmly realistic, even skeptical, of them. We are to assume the best and the worst simultaneously. Two things enable us to do this: grace and wonder.

Grace is the context in which we can love or trust or respect anyone—no matter how high or low our appraisal is of him or her. God's life-shaping grace through Jesus in the person of the Holy Spirit is our daily means of living a God-honoring and others-loving life. Every good thing that we do is by grace. Every good thing that we have is by grace. Any ability we have to love others undeservingly is by grace.

While grace is the context and the means of loving and hoping, it is wonder that balances these two incongruous demands because wonder, curiosity, is what drives our own awareness of grace. The more we dig into grace and understand it and see it and discover its secrets, the more we will be able to love the unlovable while still seeing them for exactly who and what they are. In large part this is because we will recognize how unlovable we are, how unpleasant, how unkind, how decidedly fallen. We will see the marks of grace on our lives, the way it shapes us and carries us.

We can only come to grips with our badness and God's goodness through wonder and curiosity, by being noticers of our propensity for ill and God's propensity to bless. We explore and ask and seek the depths of the riches of God's grace, and the more we discover, the more it will shape our interactions and reactions to others.

Knowing our own sinfulness puts us in a position to properly understand others too. Because of God's grace we can honestly confront the evil within us, and seeing what lies within gives a sense of what lies in others too. As I look into my heart and see the pride, lust, deceit, anger, and jealousy roiling, I know two things: *God's grace is big enough to solve that mess, and that same mess lies within every other person too.*

We are all capable of heinous wrongs. How many times have you heard of a person cheating on their spouse and said, "*Her?* I could never imagine her doing such a thing!" How many good friendships have you seen fall apart because of petty jealousy turned into bitterness? How many times have you seen news footage of neighbors describing a killer as "such a nice boy"? I am sure you know a good and decent person or three who have embezzled or stolen from their company.

You and I are no different from the cheaters, thieves, killers, and back-stabbers. If we are willing to explore our own hearts, we will see the evil there, and equally, if we are willing to explore God's grace, we will see the solution there. We are they.

We can now look at others with a clear sense of what evils they are capable of and a deep sense of hope in God's grace for them. We do not trust them, but we do trust what God is doing in them. We trust that those who are in Christ are truly new creations. We are aware that every relationship is a risk because of every person's endless capacity for selfishness and sin, but we know that God's grace makes it a risk worth taking because grace in my life added to grace in someone else's life is an exponential increase to both our benefits. We also know how little we can be trusted aside from God's work, and we know we need grace from others. It is a symbiotic relationship.

On this basis of grace we can safely turn our curiosity outward. We don't blindly walk into relationships. Curiosity and grace have opened our eyes to the risks and rewards. We can ask questions without agendas and answer them without guardedness. We do not need to be surprised by what we find in others. (In fact, surprise and shock at someone else's sin very well might indicate you haven't acknowledged your own.)

As we turn our curiosity toward the lives of others, we will begin to see more reason for skepticism but also more evidences of God's work. This tension will pull us forward. Sometimes it will be uncomfortable—we will want to give up on people and write them off, to withdraw from them and live behind a relational wall. When we do this, though, we fail to recall that God did not withdraw from us when we wronged Him. On the contrary, He reached down and drew us to Himself.

Grace and wonder are a risk. They open us up to hurt. But they are the only way to balance the twin realities that humanity is awful and we are to love it regardless. We are not fools, assuming the best and frolicking mindlessly out into the world expecting it to be all puppies and flowers and warm hugs—a curious mind recognizes this isn't the case. Neither are we purely skeptics assuming the worst about others—grace reminds us of our need and theirs and how God changes lives. Grace and wonder keep us firmly rooted in our need for grace, the immensity of grace, humanity's need for grace, and our ability to offer humanity grace because of what was given to us.

A Questioning Faith

Just as our interaction with the world is marked by tension, so too is our interaction with God. Many Christians function under a belief, either tacit or explicit, that questioning God is sinful, or at least unwise. What this leads to is the blind acceptance of whatever teaching they receive first and the inability to reconcile anything that doesn't mesh with it perfectly. I probably shouldn't be, but I am continually stunned by the number of people who accept and defend utter nonsense they hear from the mouth of a church leader just because that person is a church leader. "Well, pastor said _____" is a blanket, unassailable defense for many people—reason and theology be discarded along with common sense in many cases.

Of course, if asking questions is forbidden, most people stop think-ing altogether. They just muddle ahead in whatever theological or bibli-cal framework they were handed until life drunkenly runs a red light and smashes into them crushing the framework and leaving them with nothing but questions.

The Christian faith should be curious, not blind.

It should be full of questions, not fear questions.

Yes, faith is the acceptance and belief in things we cannot see, but that does not mean it is passive. The very nature of God should spur endless questions since He is so much greater than our understanding.

Questions that spawn from curiosity are not skeptical questions. They are born from doubt, a lack of certainty, but they are not loaded with preconceptions. A curious faith asks "why?" but does not shake its fist or stubbornly cross its arms while doing so. It asks "why?" in the hopes that God will offer a reason but with the assurance that if He doesn't (and He often doesn't), the reason must simply be for Him to know and it to trust. The questions a curious faith asks are those that draw the asker deeper into belief.

Curiosity can't exist without questions and neither can faith. Curiosity without questions is a tree without wood. Faith without ques-tions petrifies and disintegrates. As Christians we have put our faith in an endless supply of wonderment and bafflement. God will never cease to amaze the curious Christian. He will never cease to confuse and befuddle us either. We will never understand His ways, His thoughts, His plans.

At every moment He is weaving every breath from every living thing in with every thought and every breeze and every wave and every every thing to form life the universe over, all while moving us inexorably forward in His plan for eternity. We will never understand this even fractionally. But the more we try, the greater our faith will become. Asking questions in an effort to know more of God will only ever strengthen our faith and assure our doubts.

Chapter 9

How Curiosity Shapes the Christian's Life

CURIOSITY IS A CONCEPT, but concepts only matter in as much as they shape real life. To this point we've mainly looked at how curiosity shapes the mind and heart. I believe that what and how people think and believe directs and motivates their actions, but most of us still need some instruction on what to do. We have an almost immeasurable capacity to take right beliefs and turn them into no actions. We are super heroes at knowing exactly what to do and not doing it.

This chapter is an effort to point the way, to say, "Here's what a curious life should look like." As much as I would like to, I don't know you and I don't know what your life looks like so these will not be step-by-step instructions. Rather I will share characteristics and traits of a curious life through different cross-sections of a believer's life. What I hope you see is a picture of what a curious life looks like next to which you can hold up a snapshot of your life to see how they compare.

Relationships

> Love is curiosity sometimes. Concentrated wondering about the other one.[47] —Kij Johnson

Every relationship requires empathy, the ability to put oneself in someone else's experience and understand it. Empathy is impossible without curiosity.

Curiosity asks, "How do they feel?" and wonders how the other person experiences things. When they hear criticism, does it fire them up or defeat them? What experiences do they have in their history that shape their view of life and their responses to it? How do they hear me?

In short, curiosity turns us outward, away from selfishness. Our base desire is to turn every relationship to our benefit, to get what we can out of it. Curiosity, at its best, undermines this sinful desire because it locks in on the needs and interests and desires of the other person. Instead of "What can they do for me?" it becomes "Who is this person and what do they need?" Of course we can misuse curiosity to exploit others but not as we have seen curiosity to be. *True* curiosity focuses outward, away from the self.

As a relationship develops and matures, curiosity helps us see the true nature of the other person, their depth and dynamism. People change constantly, but we often settle for knowing someone well and then failing to realize that they are a different person than they were yesterday. We think we want a staid and steady relationship with a static being, so we choose to view others that way. We refuse to recognize the change in them, but in the end that leads us to boredom or resentment. We get frustrated at changes in them without realizing we too have changed. It's why so many friends drift apart or marriages fall apart. We decide we want something new and different from a relationship without realizing the same friend/spouse *is* new and different. Or we realize that they have changed and we resent it or feel threatened by it.

Curiosity not only recognizes these changes even as they are happening but also sees them as an opportunity. Every day we can learn something new about our loved ones. These are new opportunities to connect with them, to love them, to meet their needs, to see beauty in them. Instead of relationships becoming stale and musty, they are full of freshness as new aspects blow in—but only if we are curious.

> Listen with curiosity. Speak with honesty. Act with integrity. The greatest problem with communication is we don't listen to understand. We listen to reply. When we listen with curiosity, we don't listen with the intent to reply. We listen for what's behind the words.[48] —Roy T. Bennett

Curiosity is the thing that keeps communication lines open between people and also the thing that helps us appreciate them. It enables us to love better because we understand needs and how to meet them. Curiosity refuses to settle for simple paradigms and rote relational platitudes like "we just need to communicate better" or "I just need to learn her love language."

Sure, but *how*?

You don't find out by waiting; you find out by asking, studying, working. Curiosity will find out how and then explore all the ways to do it better.

Without curiosity we devolve into self-centered leeches who use others for what they offer our perverted version of happiness. But with it we learn to find happiness in making them happy, in filling them up, in helping them grow. It opens us up to their wisdom and care too so that they actually *can* offer us those things we need and those things that make us happy. For these reasons a curious friend or spouse is the best friend or spouse.

Leadership and Work

> The best leaders learn from anything and anybody . . . The greatest leaders are the curious ones.[49] —Louie Giglio

There are no experts any more, despite what people's social media profiles say. Too much change happens too fast for anyone to *really* be an expert. The business world is expanding and morphing too rapidly for any one person to keep up and master it. People can master skills, but how long and in what ways will those skills be needed? Ask CD manufacturers.

The uncurious will be left behind in the business world, both as employees and leaders.

We must recognize both that we don't know everything and what we don't know. We know a little bit about a lot or maybe a lot about a little, but no matter what there are gaping holes in our knowledge. Do we know what they are? Do we know who *does* know?

> Persistently poke assumptions.[50] —Dan Rockwell

Recognizing and owning our lack of knowledge humbles us. (Of course, if we refuse to admit not knowing, we will be humiliated. You choose which is preferable.) It allows us to gauge realistically what we do bring to the table, what we don't, and what is missing at the table. Knowing what we don't know, then, allows us to be better collaborators and team members because we seek out those who have what we don't and excel where we don't. It helps us appreciate the gifts and contributions of others. Curiosity seeks to learn all it can and then partner with those who know what we don't.

An accepted leadership adage goes "if you're the smartest person in the room you're in the wrong room." The same is true of curiosity. Even with all the right people at the table, we still can't be satisfied that we know it all. The right table is one full of people more curious than yourself. The right people are those who maintain curiosity even as they are successful. The best workers and leaders are those who are constantly exploring how others are doing their work, who is doing it best, and making note of what they can learn.

Curiosity allows us to make connections between seemingly disparate ideas to create an even better one. It helps us make connections between people who have never met but ought to be working together. Curiosity shows where the needs and opportunities exist in a market and then what drives us to find the best solutions. It is what pushes us forward instead of settling for status quo.

Malcolm Gladwell, author of several best-selling books such as *Blink* and *Outliers*, is a master of this. Through his books, and his podcast, he weaves multiple examples and story lines together to work toward a conclusion about whatever his theme for that book is. He brings together disparate parts and unlikely examples. He finds holes in his own hypotheses and points them out. He is insatiably curious in his creating of a narrative. A closed-minded author would determine a conclusion in advance and force it into a narrative whereas Gladwell allows the stories, the examples, the other contributors to his work to build their own case. In the end he rarely lands with a hard and fast conclusion but rather offers up his findings and suggests where they might point. It is a refreshing result indicative of real curiosity.

Work and leadership are much more than knowledge and expertise and even productivity. It is fairly clear how curiosity benefits us in those areas, but being a great manager or coworker or boss is a relational dynamic. Those things I wrote about curiosity strengthening relationships in the previous section enter the fray here: empathy, care, trust, understanding.

We must be curious about the people with whom we work not just about the work itself, especially if we are in leadership or seek it. The strongest teams and organizations are those full of healthy relationships. The happiest workers are those with healthy relationships. The best leaders are the ones who care about those they lead and are trusted by them and this is exhibited and bolstered by asking the opinions of others and relying on their expertise. And all these dynamics are furthered and fostered by intentional curiosity.

Ministry

Every Christian is called to be in ministry—that is, the active service of Christ's Kingdom through a local church. In America we have outsourced ministry to those in paid staff positions, but that isn't biblical. Those in church leadership positions are called to equip and train every believer for the work of ministry (Eph. 4:11–13), but each of us is to serve.

How can we serve Christ's Kingdom if we do not know the King? Ministry begins not with understanding methods or having expertise in tactics but with curiosity about the Word, about the revelation of Jesus Christ through Scripture. We follow a fathomless God, a God beyond the capacity of our brains to understand. Our curiosity should seek to match His breadth and depth, impossible as that may be. Our appetite for learning more of Him should be insatiable. If we are sparked by passion to discover more of God, we will spark the same in others; this is the start of ministry.

From this starting point, ministry becomes a combination of relationships and work, relationships and leadership. Everything we saw about curiosity's importance for these is drawn into a ministry context. It is how we care for others well. It is how we understand the needs of those we serve. It is how we draw outsiders in and step outside of comfortable customary confines. It is how we become the body of Christ as we lean on those with different gifts than us and offer them our own. It is how we learn to serve with more effectiveness and efficiency as we seek new and better methods and practices. Holy Spirit directed curiosity is the force that drives healthy ministry.

> Church leaders have so much to learn from business leaders and business leaders have so much to learn from Christian and church leaders. We should be students of each other all the time.[51] —Craig Groeschel

Most non-church staff people do not find "ministry" to be a very compelling concept or way to spend our time. That's because we lack curiosity about it and the opportunities it represents. Those who ask us to do it also often fail to pop with sparks of passion so we don't catch fire. We see ministry as a task, as drudgery, as Christian duty—not as opportunity.

But if we bring curiosity to ministry, we will see both the magnificent God who calls us to it and the multiplicity of people it reaches and affects. We will obliterate the traditional and tired borders of ministry and begin to see it as transformative for souls, for real lives, for families, for neighborhoods. Curiosity shows us the opportunity to serve and our place in it.

Crossing Cultures

The natural result of curiosity building in our lives is that we take relationships, work, and ministry and point them outward. Or rather it is the *super*natural result because God is not a monocultural God. He is not the god of the suburbs, the soccer moms, yuppies, the hipsters, the yupsters (hipster + yuppie), or the yuccies (young urban creative, as found particularly in places like East Nashville or Greenpoint, Brooklyn) alone. We see God through our lens, our culture, our language, our past experience. We shape Him in *our* mind by *our* story and try *our* best to fit Him to *our* world. But He made the world and fits nowhere. Curiosity shows us this. It turns us insular-side out.

I write this from the perspective of a middle class, white thirty-something male. Culturally speaking, I live a cakewalk. I have all the racial and gender advantages America has to offer. (If you do not believe there are racial and gender advantages for white males, I would simply encourage you get more curious. Read widely.[52] Listen closely to minorities. Be humble enough to absorb.) I am at an age, by the world's standards, where I'm old enough to be respected, but young enough to not be culturally obsolete. This means I function from a position of power as part of the majority, for the majority culture *always* has power. Majority doesn't mean numerically larger; it refers to the culture that is dominant and defines the values and expectations of society. I have the privilege to never *have* to think about other cultures. After all, my way is the "right" way.

This is equally the most comfortable place to be and the most awful. By no choice of my own, I was born into and with little enough effort I have achieved a place where I can spend every day thinking nothing of how others live, think, survive, and navigate culture. They navigate around me, not me around them. It is a place of passive superiority that soaks deep into the soul. How easy. How terrible.

This is not what God intended. One day every knee will bow and every tongue will confess that Jesus Christ is Lord. And it won't be a segregated service with one group having their preferred music style. Heaven will be fully integrated with no culture dominating any other. So what can we do to move that way *now*?

Get curious.

Just as curiosity turns us to the well-being of others in personal relationships, it does the same culturally. Of course, this is best accomplished *in* relationship. Curiosity is the bridge between neighbors of different races because it is built on genuine interest and honest questions. It seeks to *know* the other person with no agenda or ulterior motive. Curiosity allows us to humbly admit ignorance of another's way of life, perspective, or experiences and then humbly listen when they share. Curiosity assumes the veracity and validity of another's pain or joy even if it doesn't understand and precisely *because* it doesn't understand.

We can apply curiosity to outside study as well, to the macro level of culture. When we ask questions of neighbors or coworkers, we hear one person's perspective. When we read books and articles, when we look at the history of a people group, when we begin observing the scope of a culture, we see where their individual experience fits. We see them as a blade of grass in a larger field. This kind of interest is of equal importance to personal conversation because it provides context to cultural clashes (The rising tension and cries of outrage after Trayvon Martin's murder, the riots in Ferguson or Baltimore after the deaths of Michael Brown and Freddie Gray, the controversy over the Black Lives Matter movement, and more)—where they came from, what led to them, how they impact people. Without curiosity we will judge those of other cultures. With curiosity we seek to understand and then empathize.

We need relational, micro curiosity and macro curiosity to cross cultures well. It will be a lifelong effort for the same reason that curiosity in relationship is—the endless rich depths of cultures reflect the endless rich depths of the individuals who form them. We will learn to respond to differences not as threats, our default position on the unknown, but as new aspects of something God made and we can learn to appreciate and love. We can learn to trust and we can gain trust. Curiosity born out of a desire to understand the Creator of all nations and cultures will come to see those peoples and cultures as He does.

Traits of the Truly Curious

Curiosity pointed in any direction is marked by the same traits. Whether we are investing in a marriage, a coworker, a project, a sermon, a mission trip, a friendship, or a crisis, a truly curious person shares these.

Curiosity is loving because it has explored the depths of God's love. It knows its own unworthiness and how much grace was poured out in spite of that.

Curiosity is humble because it sees its own limitations and the bigness of God and His world. It recognizes that it is no better than any other person since each bears the same fingerprints of the Creator.

Curiosity is caring because it knows its own needs and how those needs have been met. It recognizes the needs in others because it has genuine interest in them as people, as image bearers of God.

Curiosity asks and wonders because it yearns to know. It asks God. It asks His Word. It asks people. It asks the books they write and the words they record. It asks because it knows its knowledge and understanding are never complete. There is always something more to learn.

Curiosity listens because there is so much to learn and it listens because it genuinely values what others say. It listens to make them feel valued. It listens because the world around it is full of music and words and phrases, and each has the potential to raise its eyes and lift its heart and spark something new.

Curiosity watches for all the same reasons it listens—watching is listening with the eyes. Every waking moment (and occasionally the dreaming ones) is an opportunity to observe creation, loved ones, cultures, news, art. Each of these offers glimmers of God's creative glory and can spark further wonder.

Curiosity is tenacious because it will never reach the limits of discovery of a single subject or person or discipline. It will never visit everywhere or hear everything. And it is tenacious in its focus as well as its appetite. It seeks to *really* hear and understand and see.

Curiosity solves because it finds brokenness and problems then sees them as opportunities for change rather than obstacles. It understands needs that exist and finds potential solutions.

Curiosity hopes because it has seen so many millions of ways God has provided and cared and loved and created. Curiosity has examined His promises and seen Him as true to keep them. So, while curiosity will never rest, it can rest in the hope of God's faithfulness.

Get curious.

Chapter 10

Curiosity and Eternity

FOR NINE CHAPTERS WE have delved into the why and how of curiosity. I've tried to show its significance in every area of life—every area of *this* life. We live a short span on the earth, a short few decades during which curiosity adds spice and depth and flavor and meaning. But then we die. Much as it makes us squeamish to discuss, death comes for us all. And what then? What does all this effort at curiosity gain us when that happens? Is there a point to trying so blasted hard now?

Can You Take It with You?

Some time ago, probably in a rural Southern Baptist church, a preacher wiped his brow, paused, glowered, then bellowed, "You've never seen a hearse pulling a U-Haul trailer, have you!?" His point was well, if melodramatically, made and has been made by thousands of preachers since. (Though, to give credit where it's due, they got the idea from Jesus. Check out Luke 12. It's never a bad idea to get one's ideas from the Son of God; just be sure to cite your source.)

You can't take the stuff of this life with you when you die. Not your house or car or kids or 401k or 403b or lake house or book collection or dog or cat (because cats don't go to heaven). When you're dead, you're gone. So what is the point of all the effort to enrich this life? Is it simply to make our few years on this terrestrial ball more tolerable and meaningful? I hope not, because even a meaningful eight decades mean little when compared to eternity.

This line of thinking is tied pretty closely to the mind-set that says we have two jobs in this life: hold on until heaven, and see if we can win a soul or three to take with us. It leads to a dislike and mistrust of culture and the world that is usually followed by separatism and distance, a decided lack of curiosity. This mind-set is the twin brother of the one we encountered earlier that fears curiosity because it is the gateway to all things worldly, that evil temptress. But the curious person, by digging deeper into God's Word and God's wishes, would see something amiss here. She would see something missing.

Heaven will not be a faraway place to which believers can escape from this earthly den of iniquity. In fact heaven will come to us one day—a New Earth, a New Jerusalem. The earth God created unblemished by sin, the one we soiled in Genesis 3 and every day since, will be cleansed of all sin's marks and healed of all its scars. The unredeemable will be burned up, but those things that reflect God's truth and glory will remain and be even better than they were before.[53] Christ is establishing His Kingdom here and we will dwell with God.

The implications of this are so encouraging, especially for the curious and those seeking to make an impact in culture. Your efforts are not in vain. You are not just filling your years only to see it all go to waste while you go float on a cloud for the next several billion eons. No, what you are doing, if done for God's glory and in pursuit of His truth, will carry *into* heaven!

True curiosity is the pursuit of truth, the exploration of God's creation and will for the world. In this way curiosity in this life is a launch pad for the next. Everything we learn of God, every soul we impact, every aspect of culture we impact for good, everything we create for His glory is preparing us for heaven and preparing this world to be the New Earth. We cannot redeem this fallen world; only Jesus can and will do that. But we bear God's image and are His emissaries. That means that we can leave bits and pieces of His image all over this world, and curiosity is how we do that. What is more, our own relationship with Him and knowledge of Him are enriched and enlarged, and this goes with us too. We don't start over when we die; we take our knowledge and love and relationship with us.

Sometimes the Sequel Is Better

Most of the time a sequel is a mediocre follow-up to the original, better story. What is next is worse than what was, derivative and unoriginal. Not so with the next life. What we have to look forward to is not just better than what we have now; it's so much better even the most vivid imagination cannot remotely picture it.

In this life every ounce of curiosity we have points toward God in some way. In eternity all curiosity goes deeper in relationship with Him. In this life there is a veil between us and the presence of God because of our sinfulness. In the next life we will live in the presence of God unhindered and unveiled. This is why heaven won't get boring.

> We will never be of much use in this life until we've developed a healthy obsession with the next.[54] —Sam Storms

We can't very well imagine eternity, but when we try we likely run out of ideas of how to spend all that time. We get bored at the beach after a week or two and get tired of a great new job after a couple years, so imagining eternity runs the risk of becoming dull too even if we can fill up the first millennia or four. What makes heaven *heaven* is not unlimited fun and games—though we will almost certainly have tons of unfettered fun. No, we would tire of those after a few centuries. What makes it a true paradise is being *with* God, fully and freely in His presence. Imagine a world unhindered by distraction or sin or pain. Imagine free access to the infinite depths of God's person and character. You can't. But in trying you may have seen that heaven can't possibly become dull.

An infinite God provides unending opportunities for discovery, for growth, for wonder, for an expanding heart and mind. Every discovery will connect to another then another then another. We will not tire. We will not run hurt. We will not run into friction or conflict. At every turn we will see and feel and hear and taste and sense something more of God and His new creation.

I have no idea what this will look like or feel like or sound like. My imagination fails me. But when I read the following, I know the sequel will be better.

> Then I saw a new heaven and a new earth, for the first heaven and the first earth had passed away, and the sea no longer existed. I also saw the Holy City, new Jerusalem, coming down out of heaven from God, prepared like a bride adorned for her husband.
>
> Then I heard a loud voice from the throne:
>
> > "Look! God's dwelling is with humanity,
> > and He will live with them.

They will be His people,
and God Himself will be with them
and be their God.
He will wipe away every tear from their eyes.
Death will no longer exist;
grief, crying, and pain will exist no longer,
because the previous things have passed away."

Then the One seated on the throne said, "Look! I am making everything new." He also said, "Write, because these words are faithful and true." And He said to me, "It is done! I am the Alpha and the Omega, the Beginning and the End. I will give water as a gift to the thirsty from the spring of life. The victor will inherit these things, and I will be his God, and he will be My son." (Rev. 21:1–7)

Every ounce of godly curiosity you have poured into this life will be paid forward to the next and then it will be made new. Every God-honoring thing you have done or made or discovered or written or said will be purified and cleansed and perfected. Every soul who met Jesus through your influence will find perfect joy, and you will get to share perfect happiness with them. Every new culture you encountered will reflect its Creator as only it can, as God designed. It will all be made new without any of the tarnish of this world.

The Least Curious Place

There's one more verse to that passage from Revelation, though, and it reveals the other side to all this—the reality for those who refuse to honor Jesus as King.

"But the cowards, unbelievers, vile, murderers, sexually immoral, sorcerers, idolaters, and all liars—their share will be in the lake that burns with fire and sulfur, which is the second death." (Rev. 21:8)

What, you may ask, does this have to do with curiosity? At first blush, nothing. What you see listed in that verse are sins against God, rebellion against His law and His offer of redemption through Christ. One other thing is woven through that list: a lack of true curiosity.

Curiosity, true God-honoring curiosity, is rooted in humility. It comes from a place of submission to God's grandeur, lordship, and infinity. It recognizes its place as seeker and subservient and His place as Creator, Provider, and King. What you see in verse 8 of Revelation 21 is precisely the opposite of this. Every single one of the people listed there refused to acknowledge their position before God, their need of Him, and the need to seek His truth. Every single one of them determined precisely who they thought God was or was not and held Him to that standard. And every single one of those standards put them in the position of God and Him in the position of subservience.

Hell is real, and it is full of the least curious. It is full of those who determined their own truth instead of seeking God's. Whether it was a conscious decision or a tacit rebellion, every single person in hell decided that they fully understood God and all He had to offer them and it was not what they wanted. So they went their own way. They rejected curiosity and in doing so rejected God. Or maybe they rejected God and in doing so gave up on curiosity. Whichever happened, the result is that they will not experience the new life.

Instead they will experience the second death. In this life they sought life by their own means in their own way and in opposition to God's. In eternity they will spend every day confronted with the fact that their uncurious view of God will not ever fulfill them. But instead of turning to curiosity, to humility and seeking, they will resent the God who condemned them to their earned fate.

Cups Runneth Over

Curiosity is a virtue and a discipline and a gift. It is a trait and a habit. It is wide and it is narrow. It is deep and it is broad. No matter how it is expressed, curiosity brings richness to both our current life and the next. A curious life is a path toward a richer eternity.

How can this be if heaven is full of joy for all believers, perfect and unblemished? Aren't we all equals there in the eyes of God and in quality of life? Yes we are, but not in every way. Sam Storms, a professor of mine in college and one of the best preachers and teachers I have ever heard, explained it like this.

Every person is a cup with a certain capacity for joy and worship. In heaven, every cup will eternally overflow with wonder and praise and joy. Every person will be completely full of joy and peace and happiness. Over the ages every cup will grow in its capacity and will continue to run over.

But not every cup is the same size. Some people will enter heaven with a thimble, others with an ice cream bucket, and a very few with an Olympic-sized swimming pool. What differentiates the capacity? What that person does in this life. Are we pursuing God, growing, overcoming sin, learning, ministering, doing, acting, imitating Jesus, and living for God's glory? If so, our capacity for enjoyment of God is growing and we will take that with us.

> It would be very difficult to draw a line between holy wonder and real worship; for when the soul is overwhelmed with the majesty of God's glory, though it may not express itself in song, or even utter its

voice with bowed head in humble prayer,
yet it silently adores.[55] —Charles Haddon
Spurgeon

No person will enter heaven without overflowing with joy and wonder, and by the time a billion years have passed we'll be quite close to equals. But how we live now matters for our eternity and for others'. The measure of curiosity we develop and the amount of truth we discover and share will expand our hearts and lives from thimble to dinner glass to bucket to reservoir. The amount of truth we display and share will help others grow. We, in a very real way, bring heaven to bear here through godly curiosity. We discover and display the wonder of God by it.

In his book *The Great Divorce*, C. S. Lewis writes of the residents of the "grey town," a tiny and dreary and, well, gray place. It is lifeless and joyless. Some of them are given the opportunity to visit a new place, a beautiful place. It is larger and brighter and more vivid than anything they've ever seen. It is magnificent in every way. Yet one by one the visitors find a reason not to stay. In fact visiting pains them. It is all too real and too much, and they opt to return to a life condemned to nothing but gray.

Even in Lewis's provocative exploration of heaven and hell, of life and lifelessness, I see the difference between curiosity and the rejection of it. I see the life that comes from pursuing wonder at every turn, the vivid colors and expansive horizons. And I see the shrunken lifeless gray life that comes from rejecting it. And I see how believers can display glimpses of that stunning new life to this graying world too. Our curiosity is a window to a new and better eternity. It brings that eternity here.

By pursuing godly curiosity in all of life, Christians bring bits of heaven to earth. And when our time comes to die, we will bring bits of this earth to heaven as well. Which bits? We will know for certain when we get there, but now is the time to start finding out.

Chapter 11

How to Live a Curious Life

And one thing I know about curiosity: it's democratic. Anyone, anywhere, of any age or education level, can use it.[56] —Brian Grazer

I LOVE CONCEPTS AND ideas. They energize me. But at some point ideas must be broken down into workable pieces, bits that people can *do* something with; otherwise they aren't worth much. You just read ten chapters of ideas. Yes, there were examples and a few stories scattered throughout but not much in the way of instruction. So this is my best effort at telling you how to *do* curiosity.

Curiosity doesn't have a recipe. It's not like baking cookies. If it was, it wouldn't be very curious, would it?

Curiosity differs for everyone. Some people are finders and connectors. Some people are miners who go deep on a single subject and drill to great depths. Both need the other and benefit from their respective differences. For some people, curiosity is highly relational; for some it's actionable, and for some it's conceptual. Again, each is good and according to the gifts and propensities God has given them. The list that follows seeks to offer practical steps for curiosity of any cut, color, or kind.

Be Interested

If you believe the world is uninteresting, it will be for you. And you will miss everything amazing going on around you. You will miss all the amazing people and ideas and natural occurrences and creation. To be interested is a decision because our natural inclination is to shrink life to something manageable whereas being interested expands life dramatically. We must assume that God did not make a boring world. To assume He did would be to dishonor Him. And if He didn't make a boring world, who are we to live as if it were not worth our attention? Make the decision to tune in.

Be Humble

Do not assume anyone or anything has nothing to offer you. If God made it, then it has value; and if it is a person, then he or she bears God's imprint the same as you. It is arrogance to treat anyone or anything as valueless and uninteresting. If, then, all created things have value and hold interest, we should ask questions, and only humble people are free to do this. Asking questions is an admission of ignorance and a tacit statement of need. Pride abhors this stance. Proud people are embarrassed to ask questions and to look vulnerable. Pride kills curiosity more quickly than anything. So foster humility by constantly looking at the expanse of God, His creation, and all you don't yet know about it.

Look

Looking is not the same as seeing. Seeing develops with time, like an infant learning to track a parent's finger then see a face then see the room. Looking is the intentional exercise of doing just that—viewing the world, glancing about, seeing what there is to see. It is a habit of trying to see . . . something. You know it is there—whatever *it* is—because you know God made a complex, fascinating world and it never fails to offer something about which to be curious. Before you can notice, you must be looking; so make a habit of it. Look at the people around you, the weather, the architecture of your city, the topography of your county, something. Try to notice something you've missed day in and day out on your commute to work or in your neighborhood—the neighbor's funky window shades, that office building just off the freeway that looks like a prison, how the flow of traffic differs at 6:00 a.m. versus 6:30 a.m. Until you begin looking and noticing things of little significance, you'll never develop the ability to see more significant things.

Listen

Listening is looking with your ears. It is tuning in to the voices and the soundtrack and sound effects of your world. Every day you hear thousands of words and noises. You hear phrases that are funny, but you don't notice them. You hear accents, but you can't place them or imitate them. You hear sirens but don't know if they're from a fire engine or a police car. A snippet of information or an inspirational quote rolls right out of that podcast and past you because you tuned out. The old guy at the table next to you at the diner has the funniest figures of speech, but none that come to mind right now. A coworker told a really funny story, like so funny your ribs hurt from laughing, about . . . something. Every morning you walk to your car and miss the song the dove is singing or the breeze is playing. You need to develop the habit of listening the same way you develop the habit of looking. Too much is happening around you not to notice and tune in.

Record

We have terrible memories. How many times have you told yourself, "I'll take care of that when I get home from work" only to forget that you had anything to take care of, let alone what it was? How often do you walk into a room to do something, but what was it again? All the looking and listening will accomplish nothing at all unless we take note of it, or should I say take *notes* of it. Write down your observations. Use your phone or a notebook or a napkin or something. I use Evernote on my phone and computer or Apple's Notes app. They are my preference because they're easy and they sync between devices. In *Bird by Bird*, Anne Lamott writes about always taking note cards with her to jot down things that catch her ear or eye—a scene, a phrase, a sound. Regardless of your method or the implements you use, just take notes. The more you write, the more you will notice and the more you will remember, which will lead to *connections* between observations. That's when curiosity becomes fruitful beyond simply the collection of disparate observations.

Ask

Questions are the currency of curiosity. But unlike other currency there is no withdrawal limit and they multiply themselves. Spend liberally. Do not be embarrassed to ask; remember that asking someone an honest question (assuming you aren't interrupting or otherwise being rude) shows respect to their expertise and their personal story. Asking someone a question honors them, so ask away. Ask individuals so you can hear their perspectives. Ask experts so you can hear the details and depth. Ask resources (books, Google, documentaries, etc.) to get facts. Ask yourself to see if you really understand and where your blind spots are. In any situation come with a few questions prepared. They can even be stock questions for new people you meet. I promise that if you bring a few decent, interested questions and ask them humbly, more questions will reveal themselves and answers will be forthcoming.

Go and Explore

It takes a conscientious decision to step outside our lane, to get out of the wheel rut our life rolls down. But curiosity demands it. Otherwise our discoveries will be limited to our daily life and be relegated to mere ideas because we can do nothing about them. Exploring might mean crossing the street or it might mean crossing the ocean. What it *must* mean is stretching ourselves and likely getting uncomfortable. Some people will travel the world, but many people simply need to discover other neighborhoods in their own city. Going means saying yes to new opportunities—a job or position, a short-term mission trip, white-water rafting, a new Vietnamese restaurant, deep-sea fishing, playing tennis for the first time. *New* is scary for many of us, but we must remember that we are curious in pursuit of God's truth and in pursuit of connecting other people to it as well. That hope and aim will overcome much fear.

Try Things

Trying is like exploring but can be done much closer to home. It is less about geography and more about experiences. Try a new recipe for dinner every week or two, maybe something Indian or Vietnamese or otherwise outside your normal palate. Try conversing with neighbors you've waved to but never engaged. Try listening to a new band or reading a new genre of books. Try a new hobby. Commit to it; don't just test it out once. Try until you learn or have an experience to record. The easiest thing in life is to fall into a pattern of life that becomes stale. Trying things keeps things fresh without demanding a passport or mountain climbing gear.

Read

Books are a universe unto themselves. They transport readers to different times and places, to worlds that exist only in an imagination, to the life of another person altogether, to concepts and ideas. Books are information and stories and inspiration and instruction. I am preaching to the choir here since you, dear reader, are a reader. But I simply do not understand people who do not read (or listen if reading is a particular hardship as in the case of dyslexia). To not read is to the mind as not eating is to the body. If you have not been a regular reader, that is okay! Start somewhere and build. Each year seek to read a little more than you did the year before. Try to read a few minutes a day, maybe ten or fifteen. You will find that you consume far more pages and books than you imagined possible. Don't worry about people who write "The Top Fifty Books I Read Last Year" blog posts. Just compete with yourself, to improve, to absorb, to consume. And try different genres. If you love nonfiction, mix in a novel. If you love fiction, mix in a biography. If you love war history, mix in theology. If you love theology, mix in a business book. Feed your mind a balanced diet so it can grow healthy and strong.

What Else?

This is one of the most important questions of a curious mind. Always ask, "What else is there?" It is the mental equivalent of continuing to look and listen and explore and try. It keeps the door open for further discovery. And it acknowledges that God's creations—human or otherwise—are always more complex and amazing than we initially see. Asking "What else?" allows us to find connections between people or ideas that we might have otherwise missed. It drives us deeper, so for the miner it pushes further into a subject to find its hidden depths. There is always a "next," whether it means going deeper or going broader, going further in on a subject or moving to another one. The most important benefit of this question is that it keeps us from stagnating. Curiosity cannot come to a stop or it will die. It either progresses or diminishes, and "What else?" keeps curiosity moving.

Concentric Circles

Curiosity as a concept is overwhelming because it can point any direction and start seemingly anywhere. If someone is trying to develop curious habits, the best place to do so is close to home. The best thing to do is to apply the previous habits in your own life, relationships, home, and family and then work outward. You will find two significant benefits from this pattern. First is that it is more manageable and fits inside the life you already lead. You don't have to dramatically change everything. The second major benefit is that it will bring growth and vibrancy to your world. You cannot change the other side of the world by becoming curious about it, but you can change the world of your family and friends and coworkers. You can change your culture even if you can't change America's culture. You have thousands of touchpoints with people and places. Curiosity about them will bring God's truth to bear there, where you are. From there you work outward in your town, your state, your country.

Always Return to Scripture

Curiosity is about God and for God. It is an expression of worship and it honors Him by exploring the depths and breadth of His creation and nature. If we are to do something that honors God, then we must know Him, and Scripture is where He reveals Himself, where He tells what we need to know for a right and vibrant relationship with Him. For this reason Scripture is where our curiosity should be directed first and most consistently, not as a book or a text or a resource but as a revelation of our Creator. We should apply every step—look, listen, record, ask, explore, try, and read—to it with rigor and constancy. Without Scripture all our other curiosity is at great risk of pursuing falsehood. Scripture is our plumb line, our compass. Every discovery we make can be stacked up against it to gauge truth or falsehood. Of course Scripture does not have explicit words on all things science, entertainment, and culture. But it tells us all we need to know of souls, attitudes, and God's character to judge right from wrong and healthy from unhealthy. So we must, *must*, return to it time and again.

As I said at the beginning, this is not a recipe for curiosity. These are elements of curiosity, ingredients which can be mixed in various quantities with two exceptions: we must always be humble and we must always rely on Scripture. Other than those two, mix and match and sequence and build. This is not a step-by-step process, though some ingredients are more foundational for the beginner than others. My simple hope is that what I have offered here will prove to be some practical entry ways and encouragements for the person seeking to become more intentionally curious.

Notes

1. Mortimer J. Adler and Charles Van Doren, *How to Read a Book: The Classic Guide to Intelligent Reading* (New York, NY: Touchstone, 1972), 265.

2. C. S. Lewis, "On Three Ways of Writing for Children," in *Of Other Worlds: Essays and Stories*, ed. Walter Hooper (New York, NY: Harcourt, Brace & World, 1967), 25.

3. Ibid.

4. C. S. Lewis, "Essays Presented to Charles Williams," in *Essential C. S. Lewis* (New York, NY: Harcourt, Brace & World, 1967), 508.

5. Alex Osborn, *Unlocking Your Creative Power* (New York, NY: Rowman & Littlefield, 2009), 128.

6. Duncan Bruce and Geoff Crook, *The Dream Café* (West Sussex, UK: Wiley, 2015), 79.

7. Larry Chang, *Wisdom for the Soul* (Washington, D.C.: Gnosophia Publishers, 2006), 254.

8. M. P. Singh, *Quote Unquote* (New Delhi: Lotus Books, 2006), 236.

9. William Duggan, *Strategic Intuition* (New York, NY: Columbia Business School, 2007), 102.

10. From Andy Stanley's Keynote talk at Catalyst East 2015.

11. Daniel Taylor, *Tell Me a Story* (Arden Hills, MN: Bog Walk Press, 2001), 116.

12. For a helpful introduction to common grace, its basics, and its practical implications, read *Wisdom and Wonder* (Christian Library's Press, 2011) by Abraham Kuyper.

13. Joe Rigney, *The Things of Earth* (Wheaton, IL: Crossway Books, 2015), 71.

14. Ibid., 84.

15. Ian Leslie, *Curious* (New York, NY: Basic Books, 2014), 145.

16. *The Mentalist*, season seven, episode 5.

17. C. S. Lewis, *The Four Loves* (New York, NY: Harcourt Brace, 1960), 78.

18. John Maxwell, 5 Leadership Questions Podcast.

19. *Princeton Theological Review,* Volume 14 (Princeton, NJ: Princeton University Press, 1916), 104.

20. Eleanor Roosevelt, *Today's Health*, October 1966.

21. Melvin B. Greer, *21st Century Leadership* (Bloomington, IN: iUniverse LLC, 2013), 71.

22. M. P. Singh, *Quote Unquote* (New Delhi: Lotus Books, 2006), 189.

23. Smiley Blanton, *Love or Perish* (New York, NY: Simon and Schuster, 1956).

24. Stanley Hauerwas, "Sex and Politics: Bertrand Russell and Human Sexuality," *Christian Century*, April 1978.

25. Dallas Willard, *The Divine Conspiracy* (New York, NY: Harper Collins, 1998).

26. Susan Ratcliffe, *Little Oxford Book of Quotations* (New York, NY: Oxford University Press, 2012), 163.

27. Carey Nieuwhof, 5 Leadership Questions Podcast.

28. Albert Einstein, *Einstein on Politics* (Princeton, NJ: Princeton University Press, 2007), 229.

29. Joe Coscarelli, "The Aaron Swartz Reader: In His Own Words," NyMag.com, January 2013.

30. Craig Groeschel, 5 Leadership Questions Podcast.

31. Dr. Seuss, *I Can Read with My Eyes Shut* (New York, NY: Random House, 1978), 27.

32. Charles William Eliot, *The Durable Satisfactions of Life* (Miami, FL: HardPress, 2014).

33. Paul McCartney, The Nerdist Podcast.

34. Dallas Willard, *The Divine Conspiracy* (New York, NY: HarperCollins, 1998).

35. John Maxwell, 5 Leadership Questions Podcast.

36. Charles J. Stewart and H. B. Kendall, *On Speech and Speakers* (New York, NY: Holt Rinehart & Winston, 1968).

37. Sebastian Junger, *The Tim Ferriss Show*.

38. Strengths Finder is a test that categorizes one's top five areas of strength along with a detailed analysis and description of them. It is very helpful in determining how one might fit in a particular work role. It can be found at https://www.gallupstrengthscenter.com.

39. The Myers-Briggs evaluation is one of the most foundational personality tests, laying one's personality into categories in order to give explanation and reasons for propensities and behaviors. It is particularly helpful in understanding why one reacts to different kinds of people and situations a certain way. Find out more at http://www.myersbriggs.org.

40. C. Peter Wagner, *Discover Your Spiritual Gifts: The Easy-to-Use Guide That Helps You Identify and Understand Your Unique God-Given Spiritual Gifts* (Ada, MI: Chosen Books, 2012).

41. Simon Sinek, 5 Leadership Questions Podcast.

42. Brian Grazer and Charles Fishman, *A Curious Mind* (New York, NY: Simon and Schuster, 2015), 3.

43. Andy Stanley, Keynote Address, Catalyst East 2015.

44. James Stephens, *The Crock of Gold* (London, UK: Forgotten Books, 2007).

45. Samuel Johnson, *The Works of Samuel Johnson: The Rambler* (n.p., 1820). 59.

46. John Irving, *A Prayer for Owen Meany* (New York, NY: HarperCollins, 1989).

47. Kij Johnson, *The Fox Woman* (New York, NY: Tom Doherty Associates, 2000), 120.

48. Roy T. Bennett, *The Light in the Heart* (Roy Bennett, 2016).

49. Louie Giglio, 5 Leadership Questions Podcast.

50. "7 Practices of Curious Leaders," 2015, https://leadershipfreak .wordpress.com/2015/11/18/the-7-practices-of-curious-leaders.

51. Craig Groeschel, 5 Leadership Questions Podcast.

52. Some reading suggestions on race in America and in the church:
> *Under Our Skin* by Benjamin Watson
> *The New Jim Crow* by Michelle Alexander
> *Bloodlines* by John Piper
> *Oneness Embraced* by Tony Evans
> *United* by Trillia Newbell
> *Between the World and Me* by Ta-Nehisi Coates

Also listen to *This American Life: The Problem We All Live With*, parts 1 and 2, http://www.thisamericanlife.org/radio-archives/episode/562 /the-problem-we-all-live-with?act=1.

53. For a more full treatment of this idea, read *Culture Making* by Andy Crouch.

54. "Joy's Eternal Increase: Edwards on the Beauty of Heaven," 2003, http://www.desiringgod.org/messages/joys-eternal-increase-edwards-on -the-beauty-of-heaven.

55. Charles Spurgeon, *Morning and Evening* (Wheaton, IL: Crossway, 2003), January 26.

56. Brian Grazer and Charles Fishman, *A Curious Mind* (New York, NY: Simon and Schuster, 2015).